ANTI-INFLAMMATORY COOKBOOK 2022

MANY DELICIOUS RECIPES TO BOOST YOUR HEALTH

HANNA PAULSON

Table of Contents

Meatball Taco Bowls Ingredients: 16
Directions: 17
Avocado Pesto Zoodles With Salmon Servings: 4 19
Ingredients: 19
Directions: 19
Turmeric-spiced Sweet Potatoes, Apple, And Onion With Chicken 21
Ingredients: 21
Seared Herbed Salmon Steak Servings: 4 23
Ingredients: 23
Directions: 23
Tofu And Italian-seasoned Summer Vegetables Servings: 4 25
Ingredients: 25
Directions: 25
Strawberry And Goat Cheese Salad Ingredients: 27
Directions: 27
Turmeric Cauliflower And Cod Stew Servings: 4 29
Ingredients: 29
Directions: 29
Walnuts And Asparagus Delight Servings: 4 31
Ingredients: 31
Directions: 31
Alfredo Zucchini Pasta Ingredients: 32
Directions: 32
Quinoa Turkey Chicken Ingredients: 34

Directions: 35
Garlic & Squash Noodles Servings: 4 37
Ingredients: 37
Directions: 38
Steamed Trout With Red Bean And Chili Salsa Servings: 1 39
Ingredients: 39
Directions: 40
Sweet Potato And Turkey Soup Servings: 4 41
Ingredients: 41
Directions: 42
Miso Broiled Salmon Servings: 2 43
Ingredients: 43
Directions: 43
Simply Sautéed Flaky Fillet Servings: 6 45
Ingredients: 45
Directions: 45
Pork Carnitas Servings: 10 46
Ingredients: 46
Directions: 47
White Fish Chowder With Vegetables 48
Servings: 6 To 8 48
Ingredients: 48
Directions: 48
Lemony Mussels Servings: 4 50
Ingredients: 50
Directions: 50
Lime & Chili Salmon Servings: 2 51

Ingredients: 51

Directions: 51

Cheesy Tuna Pasta Servings: 3-4 52

Ingredients: 52

Directions: 52

Coconut Crusted Fish Strips Servings: 4 54

Ingredients: 54

Directions: 55

Mexican Fish Servings: 2 56

Ingredients: 56

Directions: 56

Trout With Cucumber Salsa Servings: 4 58

Ingredients: 58

Lemon Zoodles With Shrimp Servings: 4 60

Ingredients: 60

Directions: 60

Crispy Shrimp Servings: 4 62

Ingredients: 62

Directions: 62

Broiled Sea Bass Servings: 2 63

Ingredients: 63

Directions: 63

Salmon Cakes Servings: 4 64

Ingredients: 64

Directions: 64

Spicy Cod Servings: 4 65

Ingredients: 65

Directions: 65

Smoked Trout Spread Servings: 2 66

Ingredients: 66

Directions: 66

Tuna And Shallots Servings: 4 68

Ingredients: 68

Directions: 68

Lemon Pepper Shrimp Servings: 2 69

Ingredients: 69

Directions: 69

Hot Tuna Steak Servings: 6 70

Ingredients: 70

Directions: 70

Cajun Salmon Servings: 2 72

Ingredients: 72

Directions: 72

Quinoa Salmon Bowl With Vegetables 73

Servings: 4 73

Ingredients: 73

Crumbed Fish Servings: 4 75

Ingredients: 75

Directions: 75

Simple Salmon Patties Servings: 4 76

Ingredients: 76

Directions: 77

Popcorn Shrimp Servings: 4 78

Ingredients: 78

Directions: 79

Spicy Baked Fish Servings: 5 80

Ingredients: 80

Directions: 80

Paprika Tuna Servings: 4 81

Ingredients: 81

Directions: 81

Fish Patties Servings: 2 82

Ingredients: 82

Directions: 82

Seared Scallops With Honey Servings: 4 83

Ingredients: 83

Directions: 83

Cod Fillets With Shiitake Mushrooms Servings: 4 85

Ingredients: 85

Directions: 85

Broiled White Sea Bass Servings: 2 87

Ingredients: 87

Directions: 87

Baked Tomato Hake Servings: 4-5 88

Ingredients: 88

Directions: 88

Seared Haddock With Beets Servings: 4 90

Ingredients: 90

Heartfelt Tuna Melt Servings: 4 92

Ingredients: 92

Directions: 92

Lemon Salmon With Kaffir Lime Servings: 8 94
   Ingredients: 94
   Directions: 94
Tender Salmon In Mustard Sauce Servings: 2 96
   Ingredients: 96
   Directions: 96
Crab Salad Servings: 4 98
   Ingredients: 98
   Directions: 98
Baked Salmon With Miso Sauce Servings: 4 99
   Ingredients: 99
   Directions: 99
Herb-coated Baked Cod With Honey Servings: 2 101
   Ingredients: 101
   Directions: 101
Parmesan Cod Mix Servings: 4 103
   Ingredients: 103
   Directions: 103
Crispy Garlic Shrimp Servings: 4 104
   Ingredients: 104
   Directions: 104
Creamy Sea Bass Mix Servings: 4 105
   Ingredients: 105
   Directions: 105
Cucumber Ahi Poke Servings: 4 106
   Ingredients: 106
Minty Cod Mix Servings: 4 108

Ingredients:	108
Directions:	108
Lemony & Creamy Tilapia Servings: 4	110
Ingredients:	110
Directions:	110
Fish Tacos Servings: 4	112
Ingredients:	112
Directions:	113
Ginger Sea Bass Mix Servings: 4	114
Ingredients:	114
Directions:	114
Coconut Shrimp Servings: 4	115
Ingredients:	115
Pork With Nutmeg Squash Servings: 4	117
Ingredients:	117
Directions:	117
Oatmeal Pancakes Servings: 1	119
Ingredients:	119
Directions:	119
Maple Oatmeal Servings: 4	121
Ingredients:	121
Directions:	121
Kiwi Strawberry Smoothie Servings: 1	123
Ingredients:	123
Directions:	123
Flaxseed Porridge With Cinnamon Servings: 4	124
Ingredients:	124

Directions: 124

Sweet Potato Cranberry Breakfast Bars Servings: 8 126

Ingredients: 126

Directions: 126

Pumpkin Spice Baked Oatmeal Servings: 6 128

Ingredients: 128

Directions: 128

Spinach And Tomato Egg Scramble Servings: 1 130

Ingredients: 130

Directions: 130

Tropical Carrot Ginger And Turmeric Smoothie Servings: 1 132

Ingredients: 132

Directions: 132

French Toast With Cinnamon Vanilla 134

Servings: 4 134

Ingredients: 134

Directions: 134

Breakfast Avocado Boat Servings: 2 136

Ingredients: 136

Directions: 136

Turkey Hash Servings: 4 138

Ingredients: 138

Directions: 139

Steel Cut Oats With Kefir And Berries 140

Servings: 4 140

Ingredients: 140

Fantastic Spaghetti Squash With Cheese And Basil Pesto 142

Ingredients: 142

Directions: 142

Hearty Orange Peach Smoothie Servings: 2 144

Ingredients: 144

Directions: 144

Banana Almond Butter Muffins Servings: 6 145

Ingredients: 145

Directions: 145

Breakfast Porridge Servings: 1 147

Ingredients: 147

Directions: 147

Banana Bread Overnight Oats Servings: 3 148

Ingredients: 148

Directions: 148

Choco Chia Banana Bowl Servings: 3 150

Ingredients: 150

Directions: 150

Anti-inflammatory Cherry Spinach Smoothie Servings: 1 152

Ingredients: 152

Directions: 152

Spicy Shakshuka Servings: 4 154

Ingredients: 154

Directions: 155

5-minute Golden Milk Servings: 1 157

Ingredients: 157

Directions: 157

Breakfast Oatmeal Servings: 1 159

Ingredients: 159

Directions: 159

No-bake Turmeric Protein Donuts Servings: 8 161

Ingredients: 161

Directions: 161

Cheddar & Kale Frittata Servings: 6 163

Ingredients: 163

Directions: 163

Mediterranean Frittata Servings: 6 165

Ingredients: 165

Directions: 165

Buckwheat Cinnamon And Ginger Granola Servings: 5 167

Ingredients: 167

Directions: 168

Cilantro Pancakes Servings: 6 169

Ingredients: 169

Directions: 169

Raspberry Grapefruit Smoothie Servings: 1 171

Ingredients: 171

Directions: 171

Peanut Butter Granola Servings: 8 172

Ingredients: 172

Directions: 172

Turmeric Oven Scrambled Eggs Servings: 6 174

Ingredients: 174

Directions: 174

Chia And Oat Breakfast Bran Servings: 2 176

Ingredients: 176

Directions: 176

Rhubarb, Apple Plus Ginger Muffin Recipe Servings: 8 178

Ingredients: 178

Breakfast Grains And Fruits Servings: 6 180

Ingredients: 180

Directions: 180

Perky Paleo Potato & Protein Powder Servings: 1 182

Ingredients: 182

Directions: 182

Tomato Bruschetta With Basil Servings: 8 184

Ingredients: 184

Directions: 184

Cinnamon Pancakes With Coconut Servings: 2 186

Ingredients: 186

Directions: 186

Nutty Blueberry Banana Oatmeal Servings: 6 188

Ingredients: 188

Directions: 189

Poached Salmon Egg Toast Servings: 2 190

Ingredients: 190

Directions: 190

Chia Breakfast Pudding Servings: 2 191

Ingredients: 191

Directions: 191

Eggs With Cheese Servings: 1 192

Ingredients: 192

Directions: 192

Tropical Bowls Servings: 2 194

Ingredients: 194

Directions: 194

Tex-mex Hash Browns Servings: 4 195

Ingredients: 195

Directions: 195

Shirataki Pasta With Avocado And Cream Servings: 2 197

Ingredients: 197

Directions: 197

Delicious Amaranth Porridge Servings: 2 199

Ingredients: 199

Directions: 199

Almond Flour Pancakes With Cream Cheese Servings: 2 201

Ingredients: 201

Directions: 201

Turkey Apple Breakfast Hash Servings: 5 203

Ingredients: 203

Directions: 204

Cheesy Flax And Hemp Seeds Muffins Servings: 2 206

Ingredients: 206

Directions: 207

Cheesy Cauliflower Waffles With Chives Servings: 2 208

Ingredients: 208

Directions: 208

Breakfast Sandwich Servings: 1 210

Ingredients: 210

Directions: 210

106. Savory Veggie Muffins Servings: 5 210

Ingredients: 210

Directions: 211

Zucchini Pancakes Servings: 8 213

Ingredients: 213

Directions: 213

Breakfast Burgers With Avocado Buns Servings: 1 215

Ingredients: 215

Directions: 215

Tasty Cheesy And Creamy Spinach Puffs Servings: 2 217

Ingredients: 217

Directions: 217

Meatball Taco Bowls Ingredients:

Meatballs:

1 lb. Lean Ground Beef (sub any ground meat like pork, turkey or chicken)

1 Egg

1/4 cup finely cleaved Kale or crisp herbs like Parsley or Cilantro (discretionary)

1 tsp Salt

1/2 tsp Black Pepper

Taco Bowls

2 cups Enchilada Sauce (we utilize custom made) 16 Meatballs (fixings recorded previously)

2 cups Cooked Rice, white or dark colored

1 Avocado, cut

1 cup locally acquired Salsa or Pico de Gallo 1 cup Shredded Cheese

1 Jalapeno, daintily cut (discretionary)

1 Tbsp Cilantro, cleaved

1 Lime, cut into wedges

Tortilla Chips, for serving

Directions:

1. To Make/Freeze

2. In a huge bowl, join ground meat, eggs, kale (if utilizing), salt and pepper. Blend in with your hands just until equitably consolidated.

Structure into 16 meatballs around 1-inch in distance across and place on a sheet dish fixed with foil.

3. In the event that utilizing inside several days, refrigerate for as long as 2 days.

4. In the event that freezing, place sheet container in cooler until meatballs are strong. Move to a cooler sack. Meatballs will keep in the cooler for 3 to 4 months.

5. To Cook

6. In a medium pot, bring enchilada sauce to a low stew. Include meatballs (no compelling reason to defrost first if meatballs were

solidified). Stew meatballs until cooked through, 12 minutes assuming crisp and 20 minutes whenever solidified.

7. While meatballs stew, prep different fixings.

8. Amass taco bowls by garnish rice with meatballs and sauce, cut avocado, salsa, cheddar, jalapeño cuts, and cilantro. Present with lime wedges and tortilla chips.

Avocado Pesto Zoodles With Salmon *Servings: 4*

Cooking Time: 25 Minutes

Ingredients:

1 tablespoon pesto

1 lemon

2 frozen/fresh salmon steaks

1 large zucchini, spiralized

1 tablespoon black pepper

1 avocado

1/4 cup parmesan, grated

Italian seasoning

Directions:

1. Heat-up the oven to 375 F. Season salmon with Italian seasoning, salt, and pepper and bake for 20 minutes.

2. Add avocados to the bowl along with a tablespoon of pepper, lemon juice, and a tablespoon of pesto. Mash the avocados and keep it aside.

3. Add zucchini noodles to a serving platter, followed by avocado mixture and salmon.

4. Sprinkle with cheese. Add more pesto if needed. Enjoy!

Nutrition Info: 128 calories 9.9 g fat 9 g total carbs 4 g protein

Turmeric-spiced Sweet Potatoes, Apple, And Onion With Chicken

Servings: 4

Cooking Time: 45 Minutes

Ingredients:

2 tablespoons unsalted butter, at room temperature 2 medium sweet potatoes

1 large Granny Smith apple

1 medium onion, thinly sliced

4 bone-in, skin-on chicken breasts

1 teaspoon salt

1 teaspoon turmeric

1 teaspoon dried sage

¼ teaspoon freshly ground black pepper

1 cup apple cider, white wine, or chicken broth Directions:

1. Preheat the oven to 400°F. Grease the baking sheet with the butter.

2. Arrange the sweet potatoes, apple, and onion in a single layer on the baking sheet.

3. Put the chicken, skin-side up, and season with the salt, turmeric, sage, and pepper. Add the cider.

4. Roast within 35 to 40 minutes. Remove, let it rest for 5 minutes and serve.

Nutrition Info: Calories 386 Total Fat: 12g Total Carbohydrates: 26g Sugar: 10g Fiber: 4g Protein: 44g Sodium: 932mg

Seared Herbed Salmon Steak _Servings: 4_

Cooking Time: 5 Minutes

Ingredients:

1 lb. salmon steak, rinsed 1/8 tsp cayenne pepper 1 tsp chili powder

½ tsp cumin

2 garlic cloves, minced

1 tablespoon olive oil

¾ tsp salt

1 tsp freshly ground black pepper

Directions:

1. Preheat the oven to 350 degrees F.

2. In a bowl, combine cayenne pepper, chili powder, cumin, salt, and black pepper. Set aside.

3. Drizzle in olive oil onto the salmon steak. Rub on both sides. Rub garlic and the prepared spice mixture. Let sit for 10 minutes.

4. After allowing the flavors to meld, prepare an ovenproof skillet.

Heat the olive oil. Once hot, season the salmon for 4 minutes on both sides.

5. Transfer skillet inside the oven. Bake for 10 minutes. Serve.

Nutrition Info: Calories 210 Carbs: 0g Fat: 14g Protein: 19g

Tofu And Italian-seasoned Summer Vegetables

Servings: 4

Cooking Time: 20 Minutes

Ingredients:

2 large zucchinis, cut into ¼-inch slices

2 large summer squash, cut into ¼-inch-thick slices 1-pound firm tofu, cut into 1-inch dice

1 cup vegetable broth or water

3 tablespoons extra-virgin olive oil

2 garlic cloves, sliced

1 teaspoon salt

1 teaspoon Italian herb seasoning blend

¼ teaspoon freshly ground black pepper

1 tablespoon thinly sliced fresh basil

Directions:

1. Preheat the oven to 400°F.

2. Combine the zucchini, squash, tofu, broth, oil, garlic, salt, Italian herb seasoning blend, and pepper on a large rimmed baking sheet, and mix well.

3. Roast within 20 minutes.

4. Sprinkle with the basil and serve.

Nutrition Info: Calories 213 Total Fat: 16g Total Carbohydrates: 9g Sugar: 4g Fiber: 3g Protein: 13g Sodium: 806mg

Strawberry And Goat Cheese Salad Ingredients:

1-pound crisp strawberries, diced

Discretionary: 1 to 2 teaspoons nectar or maple syrup, to taste 2 ounces disintegrated goat cheddar (about ½ cup) ¼ cup cleaved crisp basil, in addition to a couple of little basil leaves for embellish

1 tablespoon extra-virgin olive oil

1 tablespoon thick balsamic vinegar*

½ teaspoon Maldon flaky ocean salt or an inadequate ¼

teaspoon fine ocean salt

Crisply ground dark pepper

Directions:

1. Spread the diced strawberries over a medium serving platter or shallow serving bowl. In the event that the strawberries aren't sufficiently sweet exactly as you would prefer, hurl them with a touch of nectar or maple syrup.

2. Sprinkle the disintegrated goat cheddar over the strawberries, trailed by the hacked basil. Shower the olive oil and balsamic vinegar on top.

3. Polish off the plate of mixed greens with the salt, a couple of bits of crisply ground dark pepper, and the saved basil leaves. For the most excellent introduction, serve the plate of mixed greens speedily.

Scraps will keep well in the fridge, however, for around 3 days.

Turmeric Cauliflower And Cod Stew *Servings: 4*

Cooking Time: 30 Minutes

Ingredients:

½ pound cauliflower florets

1-pound cod fillets, boneless, skinless and cubed 1 tablespoons olive oil

1 yellow onion, chopped

½ teaspoon cumin seeds

1 green chili, chopped

¼ teaspoon turmeric powder

2 tomatoes chopped

A pinch of salt and black pepper

½ cup chicken stock

1 tablespoon cilantro, chopped

Directions:

1. Heat up a pot with the oil over medium heat, add the onion, chili, cumin and turmeric, stir and cook for 5 minutes.

2. Add the cauliflower, the fish and the other ingredients, toss, bring to a simmer and cook over medium heat for 25 minutes more.

3. Divide the stew into bowls and serve.

Nutrition Info: calories 281, fat 6, fiber 4, carbs 8, protein 12

Walnuts And Asparagus Delight Servings: 4

Cooking Time: 5 Minutes

Ingredients:

1 and ½ tablespoons olive oil

¾ pound asparagus, trimmed

¼ cup walnuts, chopped

Sunflower seeds and pepper to taste

Directions:

1. Place a skillet over medium heat add olive oil and let it heat up.

2. Add asparagus, Sauté for 5 minutes until browned.

3. Season with sunflower seeds and pepper.

4. Remove heat.

5. Add walnuts and toss.

Nutrition Info: Calories: 124Fat: 12gCarbohydrates: 2gProtein: 3g

Alfredo Zucchini Pasta Ingredients:

2 medium zucchinis spiralized

1-2 TB Vegan Parmesan (discretionary)

Fast Alfredo Sauce

1/2 cup crude cashews drenched for a couple of hours or in bubbling water for 10 minutes

2 TB lemon juice

3 TB nourishing yeast

2 tsp white miso (can sub tamari, soy sauce, or coconut aminos)

1 tsp onion powder

1/2 tsp garlic powder

1/4-1/2 cup water

Directions:

1. Spiralize zucchini noodles.

2. Add all alfredo fixings to a fast blender (beginning with 1/4 cup of water) and mix until smooth. In the event that your sauce is excessively thick,

include more water a tablespoon at once until you get the consistency you're searching for.

3. Top zucchini noodles with alfredo sauce and on the off chance that you'd like, some vegetarian pram.

Quinoa Turkey Chicken_Ingredients:

1 cup quinoa, flushed

3-1/2 cups water, isolated

1/2-pound lean ground turkey

1 enormous sweet onion, slashed

1 medium sweet red pepper, slashed

4 garlic cloves, minced

1 tablespoon bean stew powder

1 tablespoon ground cumin

1/2 teaspoon ground cinnamon

2 jars (15 ounces each) dark beans, flushed and depleted 1 can (28 ounces) squashed tomatoes

1 medium zucchini, slashed

1 chipotle pepper in adobo sauce, slashed

1 tablespoon adobo sauce

1 narrows leaf

1 teaspoon dried oregano

1/2 teaspoon salt

1/4 teaspoon pepper

1 cup solidified corn, defrosted

1/4 cup minced crisp cilantro

Discretionary garnishes: Cubed avocado, destroyed Monterey Jack cheddar

Directions:

1. In an enormous pan, heat quinoa and 2 cups water to the point of boiling. Decrease heat; spread and stew for 12-15 minutes or until water is retained. Expel from the warmth; lighten with a fork and put in a safe spot.

2. Then, in an enormous pan covered with cooking shower, cook the turkey, onion, red pepper and garlic over medium warmth until meat is never again pink and vegetables are delicate; channel. Mix in the bean stew powder, cumin and cinnamon; cook 2 minutes longer.

Whenever wanted, present with discretionary garnishes.

3. Include the dark beans, tomatoes, zucchini, chipotle pepper, adobo sauce, sound leaf, oregano, salt, pepper and remaining water.

Heat to the point of boiling. Diminish heat; spread and stew for 30

minutes. Mix in corn and quinoa; heat through. Dispose of narrows leaf; mix in cilantro. Present with discretionary fixings as wanted.

4. Freeze alternative: Freeze cooled stew in cooler compartments.

To utilize, incompletely defrost in fridge medium-term. Warmth through in a pot, blending once in a while; include juices or water if vital.

Garlic & Squash Noodles _Servings: 4_

Cooking Time: 15 Minutes

Ingredients:

For Preparing Sauce

¼ Cup coconut milk

6 Large dates

2/3g Gritted coconut

6 Garlic cloves

2tbsp Ginger paste

2tbsp Red curry paste

For Preparing Noodles

1 Large boil squash noodles

½ Julienne cut carrots

½ Julienne cut zucchini

1 small red bell pepper

¼ Cup cashew nuts

Directions:

1. For making sauce, blend all the ingredients and make a thick puree.

2. Cut spaghetti squash lengthwise and make noodles.

3. Lightly brush the baking tray with olive oil and bake squash noodles at 40C for 5-6 minutes.

4. For serving, incorporate noodles and puree in a bowl. Or serve puree alongside the noodles.

Nutrition Info: Calories 405 Carbs: 107g Fat: 28g Protein: 7g

Steamed Trout With Red Bean And Chili Salsa

Servings: 1

Cooking Time: 16 Minutes

Ingredients:

4 ½ oz cherry tomatoes, halved

1/4 avocado, unpeeled

6 oz skinless ocean trout fillet

Coriander leaves to serve

2 teaspoons olive oil

Lime wedges, to serve

4 ½ oz canned red kidney beans, rinsed and drained 1/2 red onion, thinly sliced

1 tablespoon pickled jalapenos, drained

1/2 teaspoon ground cumin

4 Sicilian olives/green olives

Directions:

1. Put a steamer basket over a pot of simmering water. Add fish to the basket and cover, cook for 10-12 minutes.

2. Remove the fish, then let it rest for a few minutes. In the meantime, preheat some oil in a pan.

3. Add pickled jalapenos, red kidney beans, olives, 1/2 teaspoon cumin, and cherry tomatoes. Cook for about 4-5 minutes, stirring continuously.

4. Scoop the bean batter onto a serving platter, followed by trout.

Add coriander and onion on top.

5. Serve along with lime wedges and avocado. Enjoy steamed ocean trout with red bean and chili salsa!

Nutrition Info: 243 calories 33.2 g fat 18.8 g total carbs 44 g protein

Sweet Potato And Turkey Soup *Servings: 4*

Cooking Time: 45 Minutes

Ingredients:

2 tablespoons olive oil

1 yellow onion, chopped

1 green bell pepper, chopped

2 sweet potatoes, peeled and cubed

1-pound turkey breast, skinless, boneless and cubed 1 teaspoon coriander, ground

A pinch of salt and black pepper

1 teaspoon sweet paprika

6 cups chicken stock

Juice of 1 lime

A handful parsley, chopped

Directions:

1. Heat up a pot with the oil over medium heat, add the onion, the bell pepper and the sweet potatoes, stir and cook for 5 minutes.

2. Add the meat and brown for 5 minutes more.

3. Add the rest of the ingredients, toss, bring to a simmer and cook over medium heat for 35 minutes more.

4. Ladle the soup into bowls and serve.

Nutrition Info: calories 203, fat 5, fiber 4, carbs 7, protein 8

Miso Broiled Salmon _Servings: 2_

Cooking Time: 20 Minutes

Ingredients:

2 tbsp. Maple Syrup

2 Lemons

¼ cup Miso

¼ tsp. Pepper, grounded

2 Limes

2 ½ lb. Salmon, skin-on

Dash of Cayenne Pepper

2 tbsp. Extra Virgin Olive Oil

¼ cup Miso

Directions:

1. First, mix the lime juice and lemon juice in a small bowl until combined well.

2. Next, spoon in the miso, cayenne pepper, maple syrup, olive oil, and pepper to it. Combine well.

3. Then, place the salmon on a parchment paper-lined baking sheet with the skin side down.

4. Brush the salmon generously with the miso lemon mixture.

5. Now, place the halved lemon and lime pieces on the sides with the cut side up.

6. Finally, bake them for 8 to 12 minutes or until the fish flakes.

<u>Nutrition Info:</u> Calories: 230KcalProteins: 28.3gCarbohydrates: 6.7gFat: 8.7g

Simply Sautéed Flaky Fillet Servings: 6

Cooking Time: 8 Minutes

Ingredients:

6-fillets tilapia

2-Tbsp.s olive oil

1-pc lemon, juice

Salt and pepper to taste

¼-cup parsley or cilantro, chopped

Directions:

1. Sauté tilapia fillets with olive oil in a medium-sized skillet placed over medium heat. Cook for 4 minutes on each side until the fish flakes easily with a fork.

2. Add salt and pepper to taste. Pour the lemon juice to each fillet.

3. To serve, sprinkle the cooked fillets with chopped parsley or cilantro.

Nutrition Info: Calories: 249 CalFat: 8.3 g Protein: 18.6 g Carbs: 25.9

Fiber: 1 g

Pork Carnitas Servings: 10

Cooking Time: 8 Hrs. 10 Minutes

Ingredients:

5 lbs. pork shoulder

2 garlic cloves, minced

1 tsp black pepper

1/4 tsp cinnamon

1 tsp dried oregano

1 tsp ground cumin

1 bay leaf

2 oz chicken broth

1 tsp lime juice

1 tbsp chili powder

1 tbsp salt

Directions:

1. Add pork along with the rest of the ingredients in a Slow Cooker.

2. Put on its lid and cook for 8 hrs. on low heat.

3. Once done, shred the cooked pork using a fork.

4. Spread this shredded pork on a baking tray.

5. Broil for 10 minutes then serve.

Nutrition Info: Calories 547 Fat 39 g, Carbs 2.6 g, Fiber 0 g, Protein 43 g

White Fish Chowder With Vegetables

Servings: 6 To 8

Cooking Time: 32 To 35 Minutes

Ingredients:

3 sweet potatoes, peeled and cut into ½-inch pieces 4 carrots, peeled and cut into ½-inch pieces 3 cups full-fat coconut milk

2 cups water

1 teaspoon dried thyme

½ teaspoon sea salt

10½ ounces (298 g) white fish, skinless and firm, such as cod or halibut, cut into chunks

Directions:

1. Add the sweet potatoes, carrots, coconut milk, water, thyme, and sea salt to a large saucepan over high heat, and bring to a boil.

2. Reduce the heat to low, cover, and simmer for 20 minutes until the vegetables are tender, stirring occasionally.

3. Pour half of the soup to a blender and purée until thoroughly mixed and smooth, then return it to the pot.

4. Stir in the fish chunks and continue cooking for an additional 12 to 15 minutes, or until the fish is cooked through.

5. Remove from the heat and serve in bowls.

Nutrition Info: calories: 450 ; fat: 28.7g ; protein: 14.2g ; carbs: 38.8g ; fiber: 8.1g ; sugar: 6.7g; sodium: 250mg

Lemony Mussels Servings: 4

Ingredients:

1 tbsp. extra virgin extra virgin olive oil 2 minced garlic cloves

2 lbs. scrubbed mussels

Juice of one lemon

Directions:

1. Put some water in a pot, add mussels, bring with a boil over medium heat, cook for 5 minutes, discard unopened mussels and transfer them with a bowl.

2. In another bowl, mix the oil with garlic and freshly squeezed lemon juice, whisk well, and add over the mussels, toss and serve.

3. Enjoy!

Nutrition Info: Calories: 140, Fat:4 g, Carbs:8 g, Protein:8 g, Sugars: 4g, Sodium:600 mg,

Lime & Chili Salmon Servings: 2

Cooking Time: 8 Minutes

Ingredients:

1 lb. salmon

1 tablespoon lime juice

½ teaspoon pepper

½ teaspoon chili powder

4 lime slices

Directions:

1. Drizzle salmon with lime juice.

2. Sprinkle both sides with pepper and chili powder.

3. Add salmon to the air fryer.

4. Place lime slices on top of salmon.

5. Air fry at 375 degrees F for 8 minutes.

Cheesy Tuna Pasta _Servings: 3-4_

Ingredients:

2 c. arugula

¼ c. chopped green onions

1 tbs. red vinegar

5 oz. drained canned tuna

¼ tsp. black pepper

2 oz. cooked whole-wheat pasta

1 tbsp. olive oil

1 tbsp. grated low-fat parmesan

Directions:

1. Cook the pasta in unsalted water until ready. Drain and set aside.

2. In a bowl of large size, thoroughly mix the tuna, green onions, vinegar, oil, arugula, pasta, and black pepper.

3. Toss well and top with the cheese.

4. Serve and enjoy.

Nutrition Info: Calories: 566.3, Fat:42.4 g, Carbs:18.6 g, Protein:29.8 g, Sugars:0.4 g, Sodium:688.6 mg

Coconut Crusted Fish Strips *Servings: 4*

Cooking Time: 12 Minutes

Ingredients:

Marinade

1 tablespoon soy sauce

1 teaspoon ground ginger

½ cup coconut milk

2 tablespoons maple syrup

½ cup pineapple juice

2 teaspoons hot sauce

Fish

1 lb. fish fillet, sliced into strips

Pepper to taste

1 cup breadcrumbs

1 cup coconut flakes (unsweetened)

Cooking spray

Directions:

1. Mix marinade ingredients in a bowl.

2. Stir in fish strips.

3. Cover and refrigerate for 2 hours.

4. Preheat your air fryer to 375 degrees F.

5. In a bowl, mix pepper, breadcrumbs and coconut flakes.

6. Dip fish strips in the breadcrumb mixture.

7. Spray your air fryer basket with oil.

8. Add fish strips to the air fryer basket.

9. Air fry for 6 minutes per side.

Mexican Fish *Servings: 2*

Cooking Time: 10 Minutes

Ingredients:

4 fish fillets

2 teaspoons Mexican oregano

4 teaspoons cumin

4 teaspoons chili powder

Pepper to taste

Cooking spray

Directions:

1. Preheat your air fryer to 400 degrees F.

2. Spray fish with oil.

3. Season both sides of fish with spices and pepper.

4. Place fish in the air fryer basket.

5. Cook for 5 minutes.

6. Flip and cook for another 5 minutes.

Trout With Cucumber Salsa Servings: 4

Cooking Time: 10 Minutes

Ingredients:

Salsa:

1 English cucumber, diced

¼ cup unsweetened coconut yogurt

2 tablespoons chopped fresh mint

1 scallion, white and green parts, chopped

1 teaspoon raw honey

Sea salt

Fish:

4 (5-ounce) trout fillets, patted dry

1 tablespoon olive oil

Sea salt and freshly ground black pepper, to taste Directions:

1. Make the salsa: Stir together the yogurt, cucumber, mint, scallion, honey, and sea salt in a small bowl until completely mixed. Set aside.

2. On a clean work surface, rub the trout fillets lightly with sea salt and pepper.

3. Heat the olive oil in a large skillet over medium heat. Add the trout fillets to the hot skillet and panfry for about 10 minutes, flipping the fish halfway through, or until the fish is cooked to your liking.

4. Spread the salsa on top of the fish and serve.

Nutrition Info: calories: 328 ; fat: 16.2g ; protein: 38.9g ; carbs: 6.1g

; fiber: 1.0g ; sugar: 3.2g; sodium: 477mg

Lemon Zoodles With Shrimp _Servings: 4_

Cooking Time: 0 Minutes

Ingredients:

Sauce:

½ cup packed fresh basil leaves

Juice of 1 lemon (or 3 tablespoons)

1 teaspoon bottled minced garlic

Pinch sea salt

Pinch freshly ground black pepper

¼ cup canned full-fat coconut milk

1 large yellow squash, julienned or spiralized 1 large zucchini, julienned or spiralized

1 pound (454 g) shrimp, deveined, boiled, peeled, and chilled Zest of 1 lemon (optional)

Directions:

1. Make the sauce: Process the basil leaves, lemon juice, garlic, sea salt, and pepper in a food processor until chopped thoroughly.

2. Slowly pour in the coconut milk while the processor is still running. Pulse until smooth.

3. Transfer the sauce to a large bowl, along with the yellow squash and zucchini. Toss well.

4. Scatter the shrimp and lemon zest (if desired) on top of the noodles. Serve immediately.

Nutrition Info: calories: 246 ; fat: 13.1g ; protein: 28.2g ; carbs: 4.9g

; fiber: 2.0g ; sugar: 2.8g; sodium: 139mg

Crispy Shrimp Servings: 4

Cooking Time: 3 Minutes

Ingredients:

1 lb. shrimp, peeled and deveined

½ cup fish breading mix

Cooking spray

Directions:

1. Preheat your air fryer to 390 degrees F.

2. Spray shrimp with oil.

3. Coat with the breading mix.

4. Spray air fryer basket with oil.

5. Add shrimp to air fryer basket.

6. Cook for 3 minutes.

Broiled Sea Bass Servings: 2

Ingredients:

2 minced garlic cloves

Pepper.

1 tbsp. lemon juice

2 white sea bass fillets

¼ tsp. herb seasoning blend

Directions:

1. Spray a broiler pan with some olive oil and place the fillets on it.

2. Sprinkle the lemon juice, garlic and the spices over the fillets.

3. Broil for about 10 min or until the fish is golden.

4. Serve over a bed of sautéed spinach if desired.

Nutrition Info: Calories: 169, Fat:9.3 g, Carbs:0.34 g, Protein:15.3 g, Sugars:0.2 g, Sodium:323 mg

Salmon Cakes _Servings: 4_

Cooking Time: 10 Minutes

Ingredients:

Cooking spray

1 lb. salmon fillet, flaked

¼ cup almond flour

2 teaspoons Old Bay seasoning

1 green onion, chopped

Directions:

1. Preheat your air fryer to 390 degrees F.

2. Spray your air fryer basket with oil.

3. In a bowl, combine the remaining ingredients.

4. Form patties from the mixture.

5. Spray both sides of patties with oil.

6. Air fry for 8 minutes.

Spicy Cod Servings: 4

Ingredients:

2 tbsps. Fresh chopped parsley

2 lbs. cod fillets

2 c. low sodium salsa

1 tbsp. flavorless oil

Directions:

1. Preheat the oven to 350°F.

2. In a large, deep baking dish drizzle the oil along the bottom.

Place the cod fillets in the dish. Pour the salsa over the fish. Cover with foil for 20 minutes. Remove the foil last 10 minutes of cooking.

3. Bake in the oven for 20 – 30 minutes, until the fish is flaky.

4. Serve with white or brown rice. Garnish with parsley.

Nutrition Info: Calories: 110, Fat:11 g, Carbs:83 g, Protein:16.5 g, Sugars:0 g, Sodium:122 mg

Smoked Trout Spread Servings: 2

Ingredients:

2 tsps. Fresh lemon juice

½ c. low-fat cottage cheese

1 diced celery stalk

¼ lb. skinned smoked trout fillet,

½ tsp. Worcestershire sauce

1 tsp. hot pepper sauce

¼ c. coarsely chopped red onion

Directions:

1. Combine the trout, cottage cheese, red onion, lemon juice, hot pepper sauce and Worcestershire sauce in a blender or food processor.

2. Process until smooth, stopping to scrape down the sides of the bowl as needed.

3. Fold in the diced celery.

4. Keep in an air-tight container in the refrigerator.

Nutrition Info: Calories: 57, Fat:4 g, Carbs:1 g, Protein:4 g, Sugars:0 g, Sodium:660 mg

Tuna And Shallots _Servings: 4_

Ingredients:

½ c. low-sodium chicken stock

1 tbsp. olive oil

4 boneless and skinless tuna fillets

2 chopped shallots

1 tsp. sweet paprika

2 tbsps. lime juice

¼ tsp. black pepper

Directions:

1. Heat up a pan with the oil over medium-high heat, add shallots and sauté for 3 minutes.

2. Add the fish and cook it for 4 minutes on each side.

3. Add the rest of the ingredients, cook everything for 3 minutes more, divide between plates and serve.

Nutrition Info: Calories: 4040, Fat:34.6 g, Carbs:3 g, Protein:21.4 g, Sugars:0.5 g, Sodium:1000 mg

Lemon Pepper Shrimp *Servings: 2*

Cooking Time: 10 Minutes

Ingredients:

1 tablespoon lemon juice

1 tablespoon olive oil

1 teaspoon lemon pepper

¼ teaspoon garlic powder

¼ teaspoon paprika

12 oz. shrimp, peeled and deveined

Directions:

1. Preheat your air fryer to 400 degrees F.

2. Mix lemon juice, olive oil, lemon pepper, garlic powder and paprika in a bowl.

3. Stir in shrimp and coat evenly with the mixture.

4. Add to the air fryer.

5. Cook for 8 minutes.

Hot Tuna Steak *Servings: 6*

Ingredients:

2 tbsps. Fresh lemon juice

Pepper.

Roasted orange garlic mayonnaise

¼ c. whole black peppercorns

6 sliced tuna steaks

2 tbsps. Extra-virgin olive oil

Salt

Directions:

1. Place the tuna in a bowl to fit. Add the oil, lemon juice, salt and pepper. Turn the tuna to coat well in the marinade. Let rest 15 to 20

minutes, turning once.

2. Place the peppercorns in a double thickness of plastic bags. Tap the peppercorns with a heavy saucepan or small mallet to crush them coarsely. Place on a large plate.

3. When ready to cook the tuna, dip the edges into the crushed peppercorns. Heat a nonstick skillet over medium heat. Sear the tuna steaks, in batches if necessary, for 4 minutes per side for medium-rare fish, adding 2 to 3 tablespoons of the marinade to the skillet if necessary, to prevent sticking.

4. Serve dolloped with roasted orange garlic mayonnaise Nutrition Info: Calories: 124, Fat:0.4 g, Carbs:0.6 g, Protein:28 g, Sugars:0 g, Sodium:77 mg

Cajun Salmon _Servings: 2_

Cooking Time: 10 Minutes

Ingredients:

2 salmon fillets

Cooking spray

1 tablespoon Cajun seasoning

1 tablespoon honey

Directions:

1. Preheat your air fryer to 390 degrees F.

2. Spray both sides of fish with oil.

3. Sprinkle with Cajun seasoning.

4. Spray air fryer basket with oil.

5. Add salmon to the air fryer basket.

6. Air fry for 10 minutes.

Quinoa Salmon Bowl With Vegetables

Servings: 4

Cooking Time: 0 Minutes

Ingredients:

1 pound (454 g) cooked salmon, flaked

4 cups cooked quinoa

6 radishes, thinly sliced

1 zucchini, sliced into half moons

3 cups arugula

3 scallions, minced

½ cup almond oil

1 teaspoon sugar-free hot sauce

1 tablespoon apple cider vinegar

1 teaspoon sea salt

½ cup toasted slivered almonds, for garnish (optional) <u>Directions:</u>

1. In a large bowl, mix together the flaked salmon, cooked quinoa, radishes, zucchini, arugula, and scallions, and stir well.

2. Fold in the almond oil, hot sauce, apple cider vinegar, and sea salt and toss to combine.

3. Divide the mixture into four bowls. Scatter each bowl evenly with the slivered almonds for garnish, if desired. Serve immediately.

Nutrition Info: calories: 769 ; fat: 51.6g ; protein: 37.2g ; carbs: 44.8g ; fiber: 8.0g ; sugar: 4.0g; sodium: 681mg

Crumbed Fish _Servings: 4_

Cooking Time: 15 Minutes

Ingredients:

¼ cup olive oil

1 cup dry breadcrumbs

4 white fish fillets

Pepper to taste

Directions:

1. Preheat your air fryer to 350 degrees F.

2. Sprinkle both sides of fish with pepper.

3. Combine oil and breadcrumbs in a bowl.

4. Dip the fish into the mixture.

5. Press breadcrumbs to adhere.

6. Place fish in the air fryer.

7. Cook for 15 minutes.

Simple Salmon Patties Servings: 4

Cooking Time: 8 To 10 Minutes

Ingredients:

1 pound (454 g) skinless boned salmon fillets, minced ¼ cup minced sweet onion

½ cup almond flour

2 garlic cloves, minced

2 eggs, whisked

1 teaspoon Dijon mustard

1 tablespoon freshly squeezed lemon juice

Dash red pepper flakes

½ teaspoon sea salt

¼ teaspoon freshly ground black pepper

1 tablespoon avocado oil

Directions:

1. Mix together the minced salmon, sweet onion, almond flour, garlic, whisked eggs, mustard, lemon juice, red pepper flakes, sea salt, and pepper in a large bowl, and stir until well incorporated.

2. Allow the salmon mixture to rest for 5 minutes.

3. Scoop out the salmon mixture and shape into four ½-inch-thick patties with your hands.

4. Heat the avocado oil in a large skillet over medium heat. Add the patties to the hot skillet and cook each side for 4 to 5 minutes until lightly browned and cooked through.

5. Remove from the heat and serve on a plate.

Nutrition Info: calories: 248 ; fat: 13.4g ; protein: 28.4g ; carbs: 4.1g ; fiber: 2.0g ; sugar: 2.0g; sodium: 443mg

Popcorn Shrimp Servings: 4

Cooking Time: 10 Minutes

Ingredients:

½ teaspoon onion powder

½ teaspoon garlic powder

½ teaspoon paprika

¼ teaspoon ground mustard

⅛ teaspoon dried sage

⅛ teaspoon ground thyme

⅛ teaspoon dried oregano

⅛ teaspoon dried basil

Pepper to taste

3 tablespoons cornstarch

1 lb. shrimp, peeled and deveined

Cooking spray

Directions:

1. Combine all ingredients except shrimp in a bowl.

2. Coat shrimp with the mixture.

3. Spray air fryer basket with oil.

4. Preheat your air fryer to 390 degrees F.

5. Add shrimp inside.

6. Air fry for 4 minutes.

7. Shake the basket.

8. Cook for another 5 minutes.

Spicy Baked Fish Servings: 5

Ingredients:

1 tbsp. olive oil

1 tsp. spice salt free seasoning

1 lb. salmon fillet

Directions:

1. Preheat the oven to 350F.

2. Sprinkle the fish with olive oil and the seasoning.

3. Bake for 15 min uncovered.

4. Slice and serve.

Nutrition Info: Calories: 192, Fat:11 g, Carbs:14.9 g, Protein:33.1 g, Sugars:0.3 g, Sodium:505 6 mg

Paprika Tuna Servings: 4

Ingredients:

½ tsp. chili powder

2 tsps. sweet paprika

¼ tsp. black pepper

2 tbsps. olive oil

4 boneless tuna steaks

Directions:

1. Heat up a pan with the oil over medium-high heat, add the tuna steaks, season with paprika, black pepper and chili powder, cook for 5 minutes on each side, divide between plates and serve with a side salad.

Nutrition Info: Calories: 455, Fat:20.6 g, Carbs:0.8 g, Protein:63.8 g, Sugars:7.4 g, Sodium: 411 mg

Fish Patties Servings: 2

Cooking Time: 7 Minutes

Ingredients:

8 oz. white fish fillet, flaked

Garlic powder to taste

1 teaspoon lemon juice

Directions:

1. Preheat your air fryer to 390 degrees F.

2. Combine all the ingredients.

3. Form patties from the mixture.

4. Place fish patties in the air fryer.

5. Cook for 7 minutes.

Seared Scallops With Honey *Servings: 4*

Cooking Time: 15 Minutes

Ingredients:

1 pound (454 g) large scallops, rinsed and patted dry Dash sea salt

Dash freshly ground black pepper

2 tablespoons avocado oil

¼ cup raw honey

3 tablespoons coconut aminos

1 tablespoon apple cider vinegar

2 garlic cloves, minced

Directions:

1. In a bowl, add the scallops, sea salt, and pepper and toss until coated well.

2. In a large skillet, heat the avocado oil over medium-high heat.

3. Sear the scallops for 2 to 3 minutes on each side, or until the scallops turn milky white or opaque and firm.

4. Remove the scallops from the heat to a plate and loosely tent with foil to keep warm. Set aside.

5. Add the honey, coconut aminos, vinegar, and garlic to the skillet and stir well.

6. Bring to a simmer and cook for about 7 minutes until the liquid is reduced, stirring occasionally.

7. Return the seared scallops to the skillet, stirring to coat them with the glaze.

8. Divide the scallops among four plates and serve warm.

Nutrition Info: calories: 382 ; fat: 18.9g ; protein: 21.2g ; carbs: 26.1g ; fiber: 1.0g ; sugar: 17.7g; sodium: 496mg

Cod Fillets With Shiitake Mushrooms Servings: 4

Cooking Time: 15 To 18 Minutes

Ingredients:

1 garlic clove, minced

1 leek, thinly sliced

1 teaspoon minced fresh ginger root

1 tablespoon olive oil

½ cup dry white wine

½ cup sliced shiitake mushrooms

4 (6-ounce / 170-g) cod fillets

1 teaspoon sea salt

⅛ teaspoon freshly ground black pepper

Directions:

1. Preheat the oven to 375ºF (190ºC).

2. Mix together the garlic, leek, ginger root, wine, olive oil, and mushrooms in a baking pan, and toss until the mushrooms are evenly coated.

3. Bake in the preheated oven for 10 minutes until lightly browned.

4. Remove the baking pan from the oven. Spread the cod fillets on top and season with sea salt and pepper.

5. Cover with aluminum foil and return to the oven. Bake for 5 to 8 minutes more, or until the fish is flaky.

6. Remove the aluminum foil and cool for 5 minutes before serving.

Nutrition Info: calories: 166 ; fat: 6.9g ; protein: 21.2g ; carbs: 4.8g ; fiber: 1.0g ; sugar: 1.0g; sodium: 857mg

Broiled White Sea Bass Servings: 2

Ingredients:

1 tsp. minced garlic

Ground black pepper

1 tbsp. lemon juice

8 oz. white sea bass fillets

¼ tsp. salt-free herbed seasoning blend

Directions:

1. Preheat the broiler and position the rack 4 inches from the heat source.

2. Lightly spray a baking pan with cooking spray. Place the fillets in the pan. Sprinkle the lemon juice, garlic, herbed seasoning and pepper over the fillets.

3. Broil until the fish is opaque throughout when tested with a tip of a knife, about 8 to 10 minutes.

4. Serve immediately.

Nutrition Info: Calories: 114, Fat:2 g, Carbs:2 g, Protein:21 g, Sugars:0.5 g, Sodium:78 mg

Baked Tomato Hake Servings: 4-5

Ingredients:

½ c. tomato sauce

1 tbsp. olive oil

Parsley

2 sliced tomatoes

½ c. grated cheese

4 lbs. de-boned and sliced hake fish

Salt.

Directions:

1. Preheat the oven to 400 0F.

2. Season the fish with salt.

3. In a skillet or saucepan; stir-fry the fish in the olive oil until half-done.

4. Take four foil papers to cover the fish.

5. Shape the foil to resemble containers; add the tomato sauce into each foil container.

6. Add the fish, tomato slices, and top with grated cheese.

7. Bake until you get a golden crust, for approximately 20-25 minutes.

8. Open the packs and top with parsley.

<u>Nutrition Info:</u> Calories: 265, Fat:15 g, Carbs:18 g, Protein:22 g, Sugars:0.5 g, Sodium:94.6 mg

Seared Haddock With Beets Servings: 4

Cooking Time: 30 Minutes

Ingredients:

8 beets, peeled and cut into eighths

2 shallots, thinly sliced

2 tablespoons apple cider vinegar

2 tablespoons olive oil, divided

1 teaspoon bottled minced garlic

1 teaspoon chopped fresh thyme

Pinch sea salt

4 (5-ounce / 142-g) haddock fillets, patted dry Directions:

1. Preheat the oven to 400ºF (205ºC).

2. Combine the beets, shallots, vinegar, 1 tablespoon of olive oil, garlic, thyme, and sea salt in a medium bowl, and toss to coat well.

Spread out the beet mixture in a baking dish.

3. Roast in the preheated oven for about 30 minutes, turning once or twice with a spatula, or until the beets are tender.

4. Meanwhile, heat the remaining 1 tablespoon of olive oil in a large skillet over medium-high heat.

5. Add the haddock and sear each side for 4 to 5 minutes, or until the flesh is opaque and it flakes apart easily.

6. Transfer the fish to a plate and serve topped with the roasted beets.

Nutrition Info: calories: 343 ; fat: 8.8g ; protein: 38.1g ; carbs: 20.9g ; fiber: 4.0g ; sugar: 11.5g; sodium: 540mg

Heartfelt Tuna Melt Servings: 4

Ingredients:

3 oz. grated reduced-fat cheddar cheese

1/3 c. chopped celery

Black pepper and salt

¼ c. chopped onion

2 whole-wheat English muffins

6 oz. drained white tuna

¼ c. low fat Russian

Directions:

1. Preheat broiler. Combine tuna, celery, onion and salad dressing.

2. Season with salt and pepper.

3. Toast English muffin halves.

4. Place split-side-up on baking sheet and top each with 1/4 of tuna mixture.

5. Broil 2-3 minutes or until heated through.

6. Top with cheese and return to broiler until cheese is melted, about 1 minute longer.

<u>Nutrition Info:</u> Calories: 320, Fat:16.7 g, Carbs:17.1 g, Protein:25.7 g, Sugars:5.85 g, Sodium:832 mg

Lemon Salmon With Kaffir Lime Servings: 8

Ingredients:

1 quartered and bruised lemon grass stalk

2 kaffir torn lime leaves

1 thinly sliced lemon

1 ½ c. fresh coriander leaves

1 whole side salmon fillet

Directions:

1. Pre-heat the oven to 350°F.

2. Cover a baking pan with foil sheets, overlapping the sides 3. Place the Salmon on the foil, top with the lemon, lime leaves, the lemon grass and 1 cup of the coriander leaves. Option: season with salt and pepper.

4. Bring the long side of the foil to the center before folding the seal.

Roll the ends in order to close up the salmon.

5. Bake for 30 minutes.

6. Transfer the cooked fish to a platter. Top with fresh coriander.

Serve with white or brown rice.

<u>Nutrition Info:</u> Calories: 103, Fat:11.8 g, Carbs:43.5 g, Protein:18 g, Sugars:0.7 g, Sodium:322 mg

Tender Salmon In Mustard Sauce *Servings: 2*

Ingredients:

5 tbsps. Minced dill

2/3 c. sour cream

Pepper.

2 tbsps. Dijon mustard

1 tsp. garlic powder

5 oz. salmon fillets

2-3 tbsps. Lemon juice

Directions:

1. Mix sour cream, mustard, lemon juice and dill.

2. Season the fillets with pepper and garlic powder.

3. Arrange the salmon on a baking sheet skin side down and cover with the prepared mustard sauce.

4. Bake for 20 minutes at 390°F.

Nutrition Info: Calories: 318, Fat:12 g, Carbs:8 g, Protein:40.9 g, Sugars:909.4 g, Sodium:1.4 mg

Crab Salad _Servings: 4_

Ingredients:

2 c. crab meat

1 c. halved cherry tomatoes

1 tbsp. olive oil

Black pepper

1 chopped shallot

1/3 c. chopped cilantro

1 tbsp. lemon juice

Directions:

1. In a bowl, combine the crab with the tomatoes and the other ingredients, toss and serve.

Nutrition Info: Calories: 54, Fat:3.9 g, Carbs:2.6 g, Protein:2.3 g, Sugars:2.3 g, Sodium:462.5 mg

Baked Salmon With Miso Sauce Servings: 4

Cooking Time: 15 To 20 Minutes

Ingredients:

Sauce:

¼ cup apple cider

¼ cup white miso

1 tablespoon olive oil

1 tablespoon white rice vinegar

⅛ teaspoon ground ginger

4 (3- to 4-ounce / 85- to 113-g) boneless salmon fillets 1 sliced scallion, for garnish

⅛ teaspoon red pepper flakes, for garnish

Directions:

1. Preheat the oven to 375ºF (190ºC).

2. Make the sauce: Whisk together the apple cider, white miso, olive oil, rice vinegar, ginger in a small bowl. Add a little water if a thinner consistency is desired.

3. Arrange the salmon fillets in a baking pan, skin-side down. Spoon the prepared sauce over the fillets to coat evenly.

4. Bake in the preheated oven for 15 to 20 minutes, or until the fish flakes easily with a fork.

5. Garnish with the sliced scallion and red pepper flakes and serve.

Nutrition Info: calories: 466 ; fat: 18.4g ; protein: 67.5g ; carbs: 9.1g ; fiber: 1.0g ; sugar: 2.7g; sodium: 819mg

Herb-coated Baked Cod With Honey Servings: 2

Ingredients:

6 tbsps. Herb-flavored stuffing

8 oz. cod fillets

2 tbsps. Honey

Directions:

1. Preheat your oven to 375 0F.

2. Spray a baking pan lightly with cooking spray.

3. Put the herb-flavored stuffing in a bag and close. Squash the stuffing until it gets crumbly.

4. Coat the fishes with honey and get rid of the remaining honey.

Add one fillet to the bag of stuffing and shake gently to coat the fish completely.

5. Transfer the cod to the baking pan and repeat the process for the second fish.

6. Wrap the fillets with foil and bake until firm and opaque all through when you test with the tip of a knife blade, about ten minutes.

7. Serve hot.

Nutrition Info: Calories: 185, Fat:1 g, Carbs:23 g, Protein:21 g, Sugars:2 g, Sodium:144.3 mg

Parmesan Cod Mix Servings: 4

Ingredients:

1 tbsp. lemon juice

½ c. chopped green onion

4 boneless cod fillets

3 minced garlic cloves

1 tbsp. olive oil

½ c. shredded low-fat parmesan cheese

Directions:

1. Heat up a pan with the oil over medium heat, add the garlic and the green onions, toss and sauté for 5 minutes.

2. Add the fish and cook it for 4 minutes on each side.

3. Add the lemon juice, sprinkle the parmesan on top, cook everything for 2 minutes more, divide between plates and serve.

Nutrition Info: Calories: 275, Fat:22.1 g, Carbs:18.2 g, Protein:12 g, Sugars:0.34 g, Sodium:285.4 mg

Crispy Garlic Shrimp Servings: 4

Cooking Time: 10 Minutes

Ingredients:

1 lb. shrimp, peeled and deveined

2 teaspoons garlic powder

Pepper to taste

¼ cup flour

Cooking spray

Directions:

1. Season shrimp with garlic powder and pepper.

2. Coat with flour.

3. Spray your air fryer basket with oil.

4. Add shrimp to the air fryer basket.

5. Cook at 400 degrees F for 10 minutes, shaking once halfway through.

Creamy Sea Bass Mix Servings: 4

Ingredients:

1 tbsp. chopped parsley

2 tbsps. avocado oil

1 c. coconut cream

1 tbsp. lime juice

1 chopped yellow onion

¼ tsp. black pepper

4 boneless sea bass fillets

Directions:

1. Heat up a pan with the oil over medium heat, add the onion, toss and sauté for 2 minutes.

2. Add the fish and cook it for 4 minutes on each side.

3. Add the rest of the ingredients, cook everything for 4 minutes more, divide between plates and serve.

Nutrition Info: Calories: 283, Fat:12.3 g, Carbs:12.5 g, Protein:8 g, Sugars:6 g, Sodium:508.8 mg

Cucumber Ahi Poke _Servings: 4_

Cooking Time: 0 Minutes

Ingredients:

Ahi Poke:

1 pound (454 g) sushi-grade ahi tuna, cut into 1-inch cubes 3 tablespoons coconut aminos

3 scallions, thinly sliced

1 serrano chile, deseeded and minced (optional) 1 teaspoon olive oil

1 teaspoon rice vinegar

1 teaspoon toasted sesame seeds

Dash ground ginger

1 large avocado, diced

1 cucumber, sliced into ½-inch-thick rounds <u>Directions:</u>

1. Make the ahi poke: Toss the ahi tuna cubes with the coconut aminos, scallions, serrano chile (if desired), olive oil, vinegar, sesame seeds, and ginger in a large bowl.

2. Cover the bowl with plastic wrap and marinate in the fridge for 15

minutes.

3. Add the diced avocado to the bowl of ahi poke and stir to incorporate.

4. Arrange the cucumber rounds on a serving plate. Spoon the ahi poke over the cucumber and serve.

Nutrition Info: calories: 213 ; fat: 15.1g ; protein: 10.1g ; carbs: 10.8g ; fiber: 4.0g ; sugar: 0.6g; sodium: 70mg

Minty Cod Mix _Servings: 4_

Ingredients:

4 boneless cod fillets

½ c. low-sodium chicken stock

2 tbsps. olive oil

¼ tsp. black pepper

1 tbsp. chopped mint

1 tsps. grated lemon zest

¼ c. chopped shallot

1 tbsp. lemon juice

Directions:

1. Heat up a pan with the oil over medium heat, add the shallots, stir and sauté for 5 minutes.

2. Add the cod, the lemon juice and the other ingredients, bring to a simmer and cook over medium heat for 12 minutes.

3. Divide everything between plates and serve.

Nutrition Info: Calories: 160, Fat:8.1 g, Carbs:2 g, Protein:20.5 g, Sugars:8 g, Sodium:45 mg

Lemony & Creamy Tilapia Servings: 4

Ingredients:

2 tbsps. Chopped fresh cilantro

¼ c. low-fat mayonnaise

Freshly ground black pepper

¼ c. fresh lemon juice

4 tilapia fillets

½ c. grated low-fat parmesan cheese

½ tsp. garlic powder

Directions:

1. In a bowl, mix together all ingredients except tilapia fillets and cilantro.

2. Coat the fillets with mayonnaise mixture evenly.

3. Place the filets onto a large foil paper. Wrap the foil paper around fillets to seal them.

4. Arrange the foil packet in the bottom of a large slow cooker.

5. Set the slow cooker on low.

6. Cover and cook for 3-4 hours.

7. Serve with the garnishing of cilantro.

Nutrition Info: Calories: 133.6, Fat:2.4 g, Carbs:4.6 g, Protein:22 g, Sugars:0.9 g, Sodium:510.4 mg

Fish Tacos *Servings: 4*

Cooking Time: 20 Minutes

Ingredients:

Cooking spray

1 tablespoon olive oil

4 cups cabbage slaw

1 tablespoon apple cider vinegar

1 tablespoon lime juice

Pinch cayenne pepper

Pepper to taste

2 tablespoons taco seasoning mix

¼ cup all-purpose flour

1 lb. cod fillet, sliced into cubes

4 corn tortillas

Directions:

1. Preheat your air fryer to 400 degrees F.

2. Spray your air fryer basket with oil.

3. In a bowl, mix the olive oil, cabbage slaw, vinegar, lime juice, cayenne pepper and pepper.

4. In another bowl, mix the taco seasoning and flour.

5. Coat the fish cubes with the taco seasoning mixture.

6. Add these to the air fryer basket.

7. Air fry for 10 minutes, shaking halfway through.

8. Top the corn tortillas with the fish and cabbage slaw mixture and roll them up.

Ginger Sea Bass Mix Servings: 4

Ingredients:

4 boneless sea bass fillets

2 tbsps. olive oil

1 tsp. grated ginger

1 tbsp. chopped cilantro

Black pepper

1 tbsp. balsamic vinegar

Directions:

1. Heat up a pan with the oil over medium heat, add the fish and cook for 5 minutes on each side.

2. Add the rest of the ingredients, cook everything for 5 minutes more, divide everything between plates and serve.

Nutrition Info: Calories: 267, Fat:11.2 g, Carbs:1.5 g, Protein:23 g, Sugars:0.78 g, Sodium:321.2 mg

Coconut Shrimp _Servings: 4_

Cooking Time: 6 Minutes

Ingredients:

2 eggs

1 cup unsweetened dried coconut

¼ cup coconut flour

¼ teaspoon paprika

Dash cayenne pepper

½ teaspoon sea salt

Dash freshly ground black pepper

¼ cup coconut oil

1 pound (454 g) raw shrimp, peeled, deveined, and patted dry <u>Directions:</u>

1. Beat the eggs in a small shallow bowl until frothy. Set aside.

2. In a separate bowl, mix together the coconut, coconut flour, paprika, cayenne pepper, sea salt, and black pepper; and stir until well incorporated.

3. Dredge the shrimp in the beaten eggs, then coat the shrimp in the coconut mixture. Shake off any excess.

4. Heat the coconut oil in a large skillet over medium-high heat.

5. Add the shrimp and cook for 3 to 6 minutes, stirring occasionally, or until the flesh is totally pink and opaque.

6. Transfer the cooked shrimp to a plate lined with paper towels to drain. Serve warm.

Nutrition Info: calories: 278 ; fat: 1.9g ; protein: 19.2g ; carbs: 5.8g ; fiber: 3.1g ; sugar: 2.3g; sodium: 556mg

Pork With Nutmeg Squash Servings: 4

Cooking Time: 35 Minutes

Ingredients:

1-pound pork stew meat, cubed

1 butternut squash, peeled and cubed

1 yellow onion, chopped

2 tablespoons olive oil

2 garlic cloves, minced

½ teaspoon garam masala

½ teaspoon nutmeg, ground

1 teaspoon chili flakes, crushed

1 tablespoon balsamic vinegar

A pinch of sea salt and black pepper

Directions:

1. Heat up a pan with the oil over medium-high heat, add the onion and the garlic and sauté for 5 minutes.

2. Add the meat and brown for another 5 minutes.

3. Add the rest of the ingredients, toss, cook over medium heat for 25 minutes, divide between plates and serve.

Nutrition Info: calories 348, fat 18.2, fiber 2.1, carbs 11.4, protein 34.3

Oatmeal Pancakes Servings: 1

Cooking Time: 10 Minutes

Ingredients:

Egg – 1

Rolled oats, ground – 0.5 cup

Almond milk – 2 tablespoons

Baking soda – 0.125 teaspoon

Baking powder – 0.125 teaspoon

Vanilla extract – 1 teaspoon

Date paste – 1 teaspoon

Directions:

1. Warm up your non-stick griddle or skillet over medium while you prepare the pancakes.

2. Place the rolled oats into your blender or food processor and pulse until they grind into a fine flour. Add them to a bowl, whisking them with the baking powder and baking soda.

3. In another kitchen bowl, whisk together the egg with almond milk, date paste, and vanilla extract until combined. Add the sweetened egg/almond milk mixture to the oat flour mixture and fold together just until combined.

4. Grease your skillet and then ladle on your pancake batter leaving a bit of room between each pancake. Allow your pancakes to cook for about two to three minutes, until golden-brown and bubbly.

Carefully, flip over the pancakes and cook the other side for a couple of minutes until it is golden, as well.

5. Remove your pancakes from the stove and serve them with your choice of fruit, yogurt, compote, or Lakanto's monk fruit maple-flavored syrup.

Maple Oatmeal Servings: 4

Cooking Time: 20 Minutes

Ingredients:

Maple flavoring, one teaspoon

Cinnamon, one teaspoon

Sunflower seeds, three tablespoons

Pecans, one-half cup chopped

Coconut flakes, unsweetened, one quarter cup Walnuts, one-half cup chopped

Milk, almond or coconut, one half cup

Chia seeds, four tablespoons

Directions:

1. Pulse the sunflower seeds, walnuts, and pecans in a food processor to crumble. Or you can just put the nuts in a sturdy plastic bag, wrap the bag with a towel, lay it on a sturdy surface, and beat the towel with a hammer until the nuts are crumbled. Mix the crushed nuts with the rest of the ingredients and pour them into a large pot.

Simmer this mixture over low heat for thirty minutes. Stir often, so the mix does not stick to the bottom. Serve garnished with fresh fruit or a sprinkle of cinnamon if desired.

Nutrition Info: Calories 374 carbs 3.2 grams protein 9.25 grams fat 34.59 grams

Kiwi Strawberry Smoothie _Servings: 1_

Cooking Time: 0 Minutes

Ingredients:

Kiwi, peeled and chopped, one

Strawberries, fresh or frozen, one-half cup chopped Milk, almond or coconut, one cup

Basil, ground, one teaspoon

Turmeric, one teaspoon

Banana, diced, one

Chia seed powder, one quarter cup

Directions:

1. Drink immediately after all the ingredients have been well mixed.

Nutrition Info: Calories 250 sugar 9.9 grams fat 1-gram grams 34 carbs fiber 4.3 grams

Flaxseed Porridge With Cinnamon _Servings: 4_

Cooking Time: 5 Minutes

Ingredients:

1 tsp cinnamon

1½ tsp stevia

1 tbsp unsalted butter

2 tbsp flaxseed meal

2 tbsp flaxseed oatmeal

½ cup shredded coconut

1 cup heavy cream

2 cups of water

Directions:

1. Take a medium pot, place it over low heat, add all the ingredients in it, stir until mixed and bring the mixture to boil.

2. When the mixture has boiled, remove the pot from heat, stir it well and divide it evenly between four bowls.

3. Let porridge rest for 10 minutes until slightly thicken and then serve.

<u>Nutrition Info:</u> Calories 171, Total Fat 16g, Total Carbs 6g, Protein 2g

Sweet Potato Cranberry Breakfast Bars

Servings: 8

Cooking Time: 40 Minutes

Ingredients:

1 ½ cups sweet potato puree

2 tablespoons coconut oil, melted

2 tablespoons maple syrup

2 eggs, pasture-raised

1 cup almond meal

1/3 cup coconut flour

1 ½ teaspoon baking soda

1 cup fresh cranberry, pitted and chopped

¼ cup water

Directions:

1. Preheat the oven to 3500F.

2. Grease a 9-inch baking pan with coconut oil. Set aside.

3. In a mixing bowl. Combine the sweet potato puree, water, coconut oil, maple syrup, and eggs.

4. In another bowl, sift the almond flour, coconut flour, and baking soda.

5. Gradually add the dry ingredients to the wet ingredients. Use a spatula to fold and mix all ingredients.

6. Pour into the prepared baking pan and press the cranberries on top.

7. Place in the oven and bake for 40 minutes or until a toothpick inserted in the middle comes out clean.

8. Allow to rest or cool before removing from the pan.

<u>Nutrition Info:</u> Calories 98Total Fat 6gSaturated Fat 1gTotal Carbs 9gNet Carbs 8.5gProtein 3gSugar: 7gFiber: 0.5gSodium: 113 mgPotassium 274mg

Pumpkin Spice Baked Oatmeal *Servings: 6*

Cooking Time: 35 Minutes

Ingredients:

Rolled oats – 1.5 cups

Almond milk, unsweetened – 0.75 cup

Egg – 1

Lakanto monk fruit sweetener – 0.5 cup

Pumpkin puree – 1 cup

Vanilla extract – 1 teaspoon

Pecans, chopped – 0.75 cup

Baking powder – 1 teaspoon

Sea salt – 0.5 teaspoon

Pumpkin pie spice – 1.5 teaspoons

Directions:

1. Warm your oven to Fahrenheit 350 degrees and grease an eight-by-eight baking dish.

2. In a bowl, whisk together the rolled oats, almond milk, eggs, and remaining ingredients until the oatmeal batter is fully combined. Pour the pumpkin spiced oatmeal mixture into your greased pan and place it in the center of your oven.

3. Bake your oatmeal until it is golden in color and set, about twenty-five to thirty minutes. Remove the pumpkin spice baked oatmeal from the oven and allow it to cool for five minutes before serving. Enjoy warm alone or with your favorite fruit and yogurt.

Spinach And Tomato Egg Scramble Servings: 1

Ingredients:

1 tsp. olive oil

1 tsp. chopped fresh basil

1 medium chopped tomato

¼ c. Swiss cheese

2 eggs

½ tsp. cayenne pepper

½ c. chopped packed spinach

Directions:

1. In a small bowl, whisk well eggs, basil, pepper, and Swiss cheese.

2. Place a medium fry pan on medium fire and heat oil.

3. Stir in tomato and sauté for 3 minutes. Stir in spinach and cook for 2 minutes or until starting to wilt.

4. Pour in beaten eggs and scramble for 2 to 3 minutes or to desired doneness.

5. Enjoy.

<u>Nutrition Info:</u> Calories: 230, Fat:14.3 g, Carbs:8.4 g, Protein:17.9

Tropical Carrot Ginger And Turmeric Smoothie

Servings: 1

Cooking Time: 0 Minutes

Ingredients:

1 blood orange, peeled and seeded

1 large carrot, peeled and chopped

½ cup frozen mango chunks

2/3 cup coconut water

1 tablespoon raw hemp seeds

¾ teaspoon grated ginger

1 ½ teaspoon peeled and grated turmeric

A pinch of cayenne pepper

A pinch of salt

Directions:

1. Place all ingredients in a blender and blend until smooth.

2. Chill before serving.

Nutrition Info: Calories 259Total Fat 6gSaturated Fat 0.9gTotal Carbs 51gNet Carbs 40gProtein 7gSugar: 34gFiber: 11gSodium: 225mgPotassium 1319mg

French Toast With Cinnamon Vanilla

Servings: 4

Ingredients:

½ tsp. cinnamon

3 large eggs

1 tsp. vanilla

8 whole-wheat slices bread

2 tbsps. Low-fat milk

Directions:

1. First, preheat a griddle to 3500F.

2. Combine the vanilla, eggs, milk, and cinnamon in a small bowl and whisk until smooth.

3. Pour into a plate or flat-bottomed dish.

4. Into the egg mixture, dip the bread, flip to coat both sides and put on the hot griddle.

5. Cook for about 2 minutes or until the bottom is lightly browned, then flip and cook the other side as well.

<u>Nutrition Info:</u> Calories: 281.0, Fat:10.8 g, Carbs:37.2 g, Protein:14.5 g, Sugars:10 g, Sodium:390 mg.

Breakfast Avocado Boat Servings: 2

Cooking Time: 7 Minutes

Ingredients:

2 avocados, sliced in half and pitted

¼ onion, chopped

2 tomatoes, chopped

1 bell pepper, chopped

2 tablespoons cilantro, chopped

Pepper to taste

4 eggs

Directions:

1. Scoop out the flesh of the avocado and chop.

2. Place in a bowl.

3. Stir in the rest of the ingredients except.

4. Refrigerate for 30 minutes.

5. Crack egg on top of avocado shell.

6. Preheat your air fryer to 350 degrees F.

7. Air fry for 7 minutes.

8. Top with avocado salsa.

Turkey Hash *Servings: 4*

Cooking Time: 15 Minutes

Ingredients:

1-pound ground turkey

½ teaspoon dried thyme

1 tablespoon coconut oil, melted

½ teaspoon ground cinnamon

For the hash:

1 yellow onion, chopped

1 tablespoon coconut oil, melted

1 zucchini, chopped

½ cup shredded carrots

2 cups butternut squash, cubed

1 apple, cored, peeled and cubed

2 cups baby spinach

1 teaspoon ground ginger

1 teaspoon ground cinnamon

½ teaspoon garlic powder

½ teaspoon turmeric powder

½ teaspoon dried thyme

Directions:

1. Heat up a pan with 1 tablespoon coconut oil over medium-high heat. Add the turkey, ½ teaspoon thyme and ½ teaspoon ground cinnamon. Mix and cook for 5 minutes then transfer to a bowl. Heat up the pan again with 1 tablespoon coconut oil over medium-high heat. Add the onion, stir and cook for 2 minutes. Add the zucchini, the carrots, squash, apple, ginger, 1 teaspoon cinnamon, ½

teaspoon thyme, turmeric and garlic powder. Stir and cook for 3-4

minutes. Return the meat to the pan, also add the baby spinach. Mix together and cook for 1-2 minutes more then divide everything between plates and serve for breakfast.

2. Enjoy!

Nutrition Info: calories 212, fat 4, fiber 6, carbs 8, protein 7

Steel Cut Oats With Kefir And Berries

Servings: 4

Cooking Time: 30 Minutes

Ingredients:

For the oats:

1 cup steel-cut oats

3 cups of water

pinch of salt

For topping Optional:

fresh or frozen fruit/berries

a handful of sliced almonds, hemp seeds, pepitas, or other nuts/seeds

unsweetened kefir, homemade/store-bought

a drizzle of maple syrup, sprinkling of coconut sugar, a few drops of stevia, or any other sweetener you like, to taste <u>Directions:</u>

1. Add/place the oats in a small saucepan and over medium-high heat. Make the pan toast, often stir or shake, for 2-3 minutes.

2. Adding the water and bring to a boil. Reduce heat to a cooker and let it cook for about 25 minutes, or until the oats are soft enough to satisfy you. Serve with berries, nuts/seeds, a splash of kefir, and any sweetener you like, to taste. Dig in!

Nutrition Info: Calories 150 Carbs: 27g Fat: 3g Protein: 4g

Fantastic Spaghetti Squash With Cheese And Basil Pesto

Servings: 2

Cooking Time: 35 Minutes

Ingredients:

1 cup cooked spaghetti squash, drained

Salt and freshly cracked black pepper, to taste ½ tbsp olive oil

¼ cup ricotta cheese, unsweetened

2oz fresh mozzarella cheese, cubed

1/8 cup basil pesto

Directions:

1. Switch on the oven, then set its temperature to 375 °F and let it preheat.

2. Meanwhile, take a medium bowl, add spaghetti squash in it and then season with salt and black pepper.

3. Take a casserole dish, grease it with oil, add squash mixture in it, top it with ricotta cheese and mozzarella cheese and bake for 10

minutes until cooked.

4. When done, remove the casserole dish from the oven, drizzle pesto on top and serve immediately.

Nutrition Info: Calories 169, Total Fat 11.3g, Total Carbs 6.2g, Protein 11.9g, Sugar 0.1g, Sodium 217mg

Hearty Orange Peach Smoothie Servings: 2

Ingredients:

2 c. chopped peaches

2 tbsps. Unsweetened yogurt

Juice of 2 oranges

Directions:

1. Start by removing the seeds and peel from the peaches. Chop and leave some chunks of peach for topping.

2. Place the chopped peach, orange juice and yogurt in a blender and run until smooth.

3. You may add some water to thin the smoothie if you want.

4. Pour into glass cups and enjoy!

Nutrition Info: Calories: 170, Fat:4.5 g, Carbs:28 g, Protein:7 g, Sugars:23 g, Sodium:101 mg

Banana Almond Butter Muffins *Servings: 6*

Cooking Time: 30 Minutes

Ingredients:

Oat flour – 1 cup

Sea salt – 0.25 teaspoon

Cinnamon, ground – 0.5 teaspoon

Baking powder – 1 teaspoon

Almond butter – 0.75 cup

Banana, mashed – 1 cup

Almond milk, unsweetened – 0.5 tablespoon

Vanilla extract – 2 teaspoons

Eggs – 2

Lakanto monk fruit sweetener – 0.25 cup

Directions:

1. Warm your oven to Fahrenheit 350 degrees and line a muffin tin with paper liners or grease it if you would rather.

2. In a kitchen bowl, whisk together your mashed banana with the almond butter, unsweetened almond milk, eggs, vanilla extract, and monk fruit sweetener. In a separate kitchen mixing dish, combine together the oat flour, spices, and baking powder. Once the flour mixture is fully combined, pour it into the bowl with the mashed banana and fold both the almond butter/banana mixture and the oat flour mixtures together just until combined.

3. Divide the muffin batter between the twelve paper liners, filling each muffin cavity about three-quarters of the way full. Place the banana almond butter muffins tin in the middle of your hot oven and allow them to cook until set and cooked through. They are done once a toothpick is pricked inside the center and removed cleanly.

This should take about twenty to twenty-five minutes.

4. Allow the banana almond butter muffins to cool before serving, and then enjoy.

Breakfast Porridge *Servings: 1*

Cooking Time: 0 Minutes;

Ingredients:

6 tablespoons organic cottage cheese

3 tablespoons flaxseed

3 tablespoons flax oil

2 tablespoons organic raw almond butter

1 tablespoon organic coconut meat

1 tablespoon raw honey

¼ cup water

Directions:

1. Combine all ingredients in a bowl. Mix until well combined.

2. Place in a bowl and chill before serving.

Nutrition Info: Calories 632Total Fat 49gSaturated Fat 5gTotal Carbs 32gNet Carbs 26gProtein 23gSugar: 22g Fiber: 6gSodium: 265mg Potassium 533mg

Banana Bread Overnight Oats _Servings: 3_

Cooking Time: 0 Minutes

Ingredients:

¼-cup plain Greek yogurt

¼-tsp flaked sea salt

1½-cups nonfat milk

1-cup old-fashioned rolled oats

1-Tbsp chia seeds

2-pcs medium bananas, very ripe and mashed

2-Tbsps coconut flakes, unsweetened and toasted 2-Tbsps honey

2-tsp vanilla extract

Toppings for serving: roasted pecans, pomegranate seeds, honey, fig halves, and banana slices

Directions:

1. Stir in all of the ingredients, excluding the toppings, in a mixing bowl. Mix well until thoroughly combined. Divide the mixture equally between two serving bowls.

2. Cover and refrigerate overnight or for 6 hours.

3. To serve, stir, and put on the toppings.

Nutrition Info: Calories 684 Fat: 22.8g Protein: 34.2g Sodium: 374mg Total Carbs: 99.6g Dietary Fiber: 14.1g

Choco Chia Banana Bowl _Servings: 3_

Cooking Time: 0 Minutes

Ingredients:

½-cup chia seeds

1 large banana, very ripe

½-tsp pure vanilla extract

2-cups almond milk, unsweetened

1-Tbsp cacao powder

2-Tbsps raw honey or maple syrup

2-Tbsps cacao nibs for mixing in

2-Tbsps chocolate chips for mixing in

1 large banana, sliced for mixing in

Directions:

1. Combine the chia seeds and banana in a mixing bowl. By using a fork, mash the banana and mix well until thoroughly combined. Pour in the vanilla and almond milk. Whisk until no more lumps appear.

2. Pour half of the mix in a glass container, and cover it. Add the cacao and syrup to the remaining half mixture in the bowl. Mix well until fully incorporated. Pour this mixture in another glass container, and cover it. Chill for at least 4 hours.

3. To serve, layer the chilled chia puddings equally in three serving bowls. Alternate the layers with the ingredients for mixing-in.

<u>Nutrition Info:</u> Calories 293 Fat: 9.7g Protein: 14.6g Sodium: 35mg Total Carbs: 43.1g

Anti-inflammatory Cherry Spinach Smoothie

Servings: 1

Cooking Time: 0 Minutes

Ingredients:

1 cup plain kefir

1 cup frozen cherries, pitted

½ cup baby spinach leaves

¼ cup mashed ripe avocado

1 tablespoon almond butter

1-piece peeled ginger (1/2 inch)

1 teaspoon chia seeds

Directions:

1. Place all ingredients in a blender.

2. Pulse until smooth.

3. Allow to chill in the fridge before serving.

Nutrition Info: Calories 410 Total Fat 20g Saturated Fat 4g Total Carbs 47g Net Carbs 37g Protein 17g Sugar: 33g Fiber: 10g Sodium: 169mg Potassium 1163mg

Spicy Shakshuka _Servings: 4_

Cooking Time: 37 Minutes

Ingredients:

2-Tbsps extra-virgin olive oil

1-bulb onion, minced

1 jalapeño, seeded and minced

2-cloves garlic, minced

1-lb spinach

Salt and freshly ground black pepper

¾-tsp coriander

1-tsp dried cumin

2-Tbsps harissa paste

½-cup vegetable broth

8-pcs large eggs

Red pepper flakes, for serving

Cilantro, chopped for serving

Parsley, chopped for serving

Directions:

1. Preheat your oven to 350°F.

2. Heat the oil in an oven-safe skillet placed over medium heat. Stir in the onion and sauté for 5 minutes.

3. Add the jalapeño and garlic, and sauté for a minute, or until fragrant. Add in the spinach, and cook for 5 minutes, or until the leaves entirely wilt.

4. Season the mixture with salt and pepper, coriander, cumin, and harissa. Cook further for 1 minute.

5. Transfer the mixture to your food processor—puree to a thick consistency. Pour in the broth and puree further until achieving a smooth texture.

6. Clean and grease the same skillet with nonstick cooking spray.

Pour the pureed mixture. By using a wooden spoon, form eight circular wells.

7. Crack each egg gently into the wells. Put the skillet in the oven—

Bake for 25 minutes, or poaching the eggs until fully set.

8. To serve, sprinkle the shakshuka with red pepper flakes, cilantro, and parsley to taste.

Nutrition Info: Calories 251 Fat: 8.3g Protein: 12.5g Sodium: 165mg Total Carbs: 33.6g

5-minute Golden Milk _Servings: 1_

Cooking Time: 4 Minutes

Ingredients:

1 1/2 cups light coconut milk

1 1/2 cups unsweetened almond milk

1 1/2 tsp ground turmeric

1/4 tsp ground ginger

1 whole cinnamon stick

1 Tbsp coconut oil

1 pinch ground black pepper

Sweetener of choice (i.e., coconut sugar, maple syrup, or stevia to taste)

Directions:

1. Add coconut milk, ground turmeric, almond milk, ground ginger, cinnamon stick, coconut oil, black pepper, and preferred sweetener to a small casserole.

2. Whisk to mix over medium heat and warm up. Heat to the touch until hot but do not boil-about 4 minutes-whisking regularly.

3. Turn off heat and taste to make flavor change. For strong spice + flavor, add more sweetener to taste, or more turmeric or ginger.

4. Serve straight away, break between two glasses, and leave the cinnamon stick behind. Best when fresh, although the leftovers can be kept 2-3 days in the refrigerator. Reheat up to temperature on the stovetop or microwave.

Nutrition Info: Calories 205 Fat: 19.5g Sodium: 161mg Carbohydrates: 8.9g Fiber: 1.1g Protein: 3.2g

Breakfast Oatmeal Servings: 1

Cooking Time: 8 Minutes

Ingredients:

2/3 cup coconut milk

1 egg white, pasture-raised

½ cup gluten-free quick-cooking oats

½ teaspoon turmeric powder

½ teaspoon cinnamon

¼ teaspoon ginger

Directions:

1. Place the non-dairy milk in a saucepan and heat over medium flame.

2. Stir in the egg white and continue whisking until the mixture becomes smooth.

3. Add in the rest of the ingredients and cook for another 3 minutes.

Nutrition Info: Calories 395Total Fat 34gSaturated Fat 7gTotal Carbs 19gNet Carbs 16gProtein 10gSugar: 2gFiber: 3gSodium: 76mgPotassium 459mg

No-bake Turmeric Protein Donuts Servings: 8

Cooking Time: 0 Minutes

Ingredients:

1 ½ cups raw cashews

½ cup medjool dates, pitted

1 tablespoon vanilla protein powder

½ cup shredded coconut

2 tablespoons maple syrup

¼ teaspoon vanilla extract

1 teaspoon turmeric powder

¼ cup dark chocolate

Directions:

1. Combine all ingredients except for the chocolate in a food processor.

2. Pulse until smooth.

3. Roll batter into 8 balls and press into a silicone donut mold.

4. Place in the freezer for 30 minutes to set.

5. Meanwhile, make the chocolate topping by melting the chocolate in a double boiler.

6. Once the donuts have set, remove the donuts from the mold and drizzle with chocolate.

Nutrition Info: Calories 320Total Fat 26gSaturated Fat 5gTotal Carbs 20gNet Carbs 18gProtein 7gSugar: 9gFiber: 2gSodium: 163

mgPotassium 297mg

Cheddar & Kale Frittata *Servings: 6*

Ingredients:

1/3 c. sliced scallions

¼ tsp. pepper

1 diced red pepper

¾ c. non-fat milk

1 c. shredded sharp low-fat cheddar cheese

1 tsp. olive oil

5 oz. baby kale and spinach

12 eggs

Directions:

1. Preheat oven to 375 0F.

2. With olive oil, grease a glass casserole dish.

3. In a bowl, whisk well all ingredients except for cheese.

4. Pour egg mixture in prepared dish and bake for 35 minutes.

5. Remove from oven and sprinkle cheese on top and broil for 5 minutes.

6. Remove from oven and let it sit for 10 minutes.

7. Cut up and enjoy.

Nutrition Info: Calories: 198, Fat:11.0 g, Carbs:5.7 g, Protein:18.7 g, Sugars:1 g, Sodium:209 mg.

Mediterranean Frittata Servings: 6

Cooking Time: 20 Minutes

Ingredients:

Eggs, six

Feta cheese, crumbled, one quarter cup

Black pepper, one quarter teaspoon

Oil, spray, or olive

Oregano, one teaspoon

Milk, almond or coconut, one quarter cup

Sea salt, one teaspoon

Black olives, chopped, one quarter cup

Green olives, chopped, one quarter cup

Tomatoes, diced, one quarter cup

Directions:

1. Heat oven to 400. Oil one eight by eight-inch baking dish.

Combine the milk into the eggs, and then add other ingredients. Pour all of this mixture into the baking dish and bake for twenty minutes.

Nutrition Info: Calories 107 sugars 2 grams fat 7 grams carb 3 grams protein 7 grams

Buckwheat Cinnamon And Ginger Granola

Servings: 5

Cooking Time: 40 Minutes

Ingredients:

¼ cup Chia seeds

½ Cup Coconut Flakes

1 ½ Cup mixed Raw nuts

2 cups of gluten-free oats

1 cup of buckwheat groats

2 tbsp nut butter

4 tbsp of coconut oil

1 cup of sunflower seeds

½ cup of pumpkin seeds

1 ½ - 2 inches piece of ginger

1 tsp Ground Cinnamon

1/3 cup of Rice Malt Syrup

4 tbsp of raw cacao powder – Optional

Directions:

1. Preheat the oven up to 180C

2. Blitz the nuts in your food processor and quickly blitz to chop roughly. Put the chopped nuts in a bowl and add all the other dry ingredients that combine well—oats, coconut, cinnamon, buckwheat, seeds, and salt in a low heat saucepan, melt the coconut oil gently.

3. Add the cacao powder (if used) to the wet mixture and blend. Put the wet batter over the dry mix, then mix well to make sure that everything is coated. Move the mixture to a wide baking tray lined with grease-proof paper or coconut oil greased. Be sure to uniformly distribute the mixture for 35-40 minutes, turning the mixture halfway through. Bake until the granola is fresh and golden!

4. Serve with your favorite nut milk, coconut yogurt scoop, fresh fruit, and superfoods—goji berries, flax seeds, bee pollen, whatever you like! Mix it up every single day.

Nutrition Info: Calories 220 Carbs: 38g Fat: 5g Protein: 7g

Cilantro Pancakes *Servings: 6*

Cooking Time: 6-8 Minutes

Ingredients:

½ cup tapioca flour

½ cup almond flour

½ teaspoon chili powder

¼ teaspoon ground turmeric

Salt and freshly ground black pepper, to taste 1 cup full- Fat coconut milk

½ of red onion, chopped

1 (½-inch) fresh ginger piece, grated finely 1 Serrano pepper, minced

½ cup fresh cilantro, chopped

Oil, as required

Directions:

1. In a big bowl, mix together flours and spices.

2. Add coconut milk and mix till well combined.

3. Fold within the onion, ginger, Serrano pepper and cilantro.

4. Lightly, grease a sizable nonstick skillet with oil and warmth on medium-low heat.

5. Add about ¼ cup of mixture and tilt the pan to spread it evenly inside the skillet.

6. Cook for around 3-4 minutes from either side.

7. Repeat with all the remaining mixture.

8. Serve along with your desired topping.

Nutrition Info: Calories: 331, Fat: 10g, Carbohydrates: 37g, Fiber: 6g, Protein: 28g

Raspberry Grapefruit Smoothie Servings: 1

Cooking Time: 0 Minutes

Ingredients:

Juice from 1 grapefruit, freshly squeezed

1 banana, peeled and sliced

1 cup raspberries

Directions:

1. Place all ingredients in a blender and pulse until smooth.

2. Chill before serving.

Nutrition Info: Calories 381Total Fat 0.8gSaturated Fat 0.1gTotal Carbs 96gNet Carbs 85gProtein 4gSugar: 61gFiber: 11gSodium: 11mgPotassium 848mg

Peanut Butter Granola Servings: 8

Cooking Time: 25 Minutes

Ingredients:

Rolled oats – 2 cups

Cinnamon – 0.5 teaspoon

Peanut butter, natural with salt – 0.5 cup

Date paste – 1.5 tablespoons

Lily's dark chocolate chips – 0.5 cup

Directions:

1. Warm the oven to Fahrenheit 300 degrees and line a baking sheet with kitchen parchment or a silicone kitchen mat.

2. In a bowl, whisk together the date paste, cinnamon, and peanut butter to combine, and then add in the oats, tossing until the oats are fully coated. Spread this sweetened and spiced mixture evenly over the baking sheet in a thin layer.

3. Place the peanut butter granola in the oven and bake for twenty minutes, giving it a good stir halfway through the cooking time to prevent uneven cooking and burning.

4. Remove the granola from the oven and allow it to cool to room temperature before tossing in the chocolate chips. Transfer the peanut butter granola to an airtight container to store until use.

Turmeric Oven Scrambled Eggs *Servings: 6*

Cooking Time: 15 Minutes

Ingredients:

8 to 10 large eggs, pasture-raised

½ cup unsweetened almond or coconut milk

½ teaspoon turmeric powder

1 teaspoon chopped cilantro

¼ teaspoon black pepper

A pinch of salt

Directions:

1. Preheat the oven to 3500F.

2. Grease a casserole or heat-proof baking dish.

3. In a bowl, whisk the egg, milk, turmeric powder, black pepper and salt.

4. Pour in the egg mixture into the baking dish.

5. Place in the oven and bake for 15 minutes or until the eggs have set.

6. Remove from the oven and garnish with chopped cilantro on top.

Nutrition Info: Calories 203Total Fat 16gSaturated Fat 4gTotal Carbs 5gNet Carbs 4gProtein 10gSugar: 4gFiber: 1gSodium: 303 mgPotassium 321mg

Chia And Oat Breakfast Bran *Servings: 2*

Ingredients:

85 g chopped roasted almonds

340 g coconut milk

30 g cane sugar

2½ g orange zest

30 g flax seed mix

170 g rolled oats

340 g blueberries

30 g chia seeds

2½ g cinnamon

Directions:

1. Add all your wet ingredients together and mix the sugar and milk in with the orange zest.

2. Stir in the cinnamon and mix well. Once you are sure the sugar isn't lumpy add in the rolled oats, flax seeds, and chia and then let it sit for a minute.

3. Grab two bowls or mason jars and pour the mixture in. Top with the roasted almonds, and store in the fridge.

4. Pull it out in the morning and dig in!

Nutrition Info: Calories: 353, Fat:8 g, Carbs:55 g, Protein:15 g, Sugars:9.9 g, Sodium:96 mg

Rhubarb, Apple Plus Ginger Muffin Recipe

Servings: 8

Cooking Time: 30 Minutes

Ingredients:

1/2 teaspoon ground cinnamon

1/2 teaspoon ground ginger

pinch sea salt

1/2 cup almond meal (ground almonds)

1/4 cup unrefined raw sugar

2 tbsp finely chopped crystallized ginger

1 tbs ground linseed meal

1/2 cup buckwheat flour

1/4 cup fine brown rice flour

1/4 cup (60ml) olive oil

1 large free-range egg

1 teaspoon vanilla extract

2 tablespoons organic corn flour or true arrowroot 2 teaspoons gluten-free baking powder

1 cup finely sliced rhubarb

1 small apple, peeled and finely diced

95ml (1/3 cup + 1 tbsp) rice or almond milk <u>Directions:</u>

1. Pre-heat the oven to 180C/350C. Grease or line 8 1/3 cup (80ml) cup muffin tins with a paper case cap.

2. In a medium bowl, put the almond meal, ginger, sugar, and linseed. Sieve over baking powder, flours, and spices and then mix evenly. In the flour mixture, whisk in rhubarb and apple to coat.

3. Whisk the milk, sugar, egg, and vanilla in another smaller bowl before pouring into the dry mixture and stirring until combined.

4. Divide the batter evenly between tins/paper cases and bake for 20 minutes -25 minutes or until it rises, golden around the edges.

5. Remove, then set aside for 5 minutes before transferring onto a wire rack to cool off further.

6. Eat warm or at room temperature.

<u>Nutrition Info:</u> Calories 38 Carbs: 9g Fat: 0g Protein: 0g

Breakfast Grains And Fruits *Servings: 6*

Ingredients:

1 c. raisins

¾ c. quick cooking brown rice

1 granny smith apple

1 orange

8 oz. low fat vanilla yogurt

3 c. water

¾ c. bulgur

1 red delicious apple

Directions:

1. On high fire, place a large pot and bring water to a boil.

2. Add bulgur and rice. Lower fire to a simmer and cook for ten minutes while covered.

3. Turn off fire, set aside for 2 minutes while covered.

4. In a baking sheet, transfer and evenly spread grains to cool.

5. Meanwhile, peel oranges and cut into sections. Chop and core apples.

6. Once grains are cool, transfer to a large serving bowl along with fruits.

7. Add yogurt and mix well to coat.

8. Serve and enjoy.

Nutrition Info: Calories: 121, Fat:1 g, Carbs:24.2 g, Protein:3.8 g, Sugars:4.2 g, Sodium:500 mg

Perky Paleo Potato & Protein Powder <u>Servings: 1</u>

Cooking Time: 0 Minutes

Ingredients:

1 small sweet potato, pre-baked and fleshed out 1-Tbsp protein powder

1 small banana, sliced

¼-cup blueberries

¼-cup raspberries

Choice of toppings: cacao nibs, chia seeds, hemp hearts, favorite nut/seed butter (optional)

Directions:

1. In a small serving bowl, mash the sweet potato using a fork. Add the protein powder. Mix well until thoroughly combined.

2. Arrange the banana slices, blueberries, and raspberries on top of the mixture. Garnish with your desired toppings. You can relish this breakfast meal, either cold or warm.

Nutrition Info: Calories 302 Fat: 10g Protein: 15.3g Sodium: 65mg Total Carbs: 46.7g

Tomato Bruschetta With Basil *Servings: 8*

Ingredients:

½ c. chopped basil

2 minced garlic cloves

1 tbsp. balsamic vinegar

2 tbsps. Olive oil

½ tsp. cracked black pepper

1 sliced whole wheat baguette

8 diced ripe Roma tomatoes

1 tsp. sea salt

Directions:

1. First, preheat the oven to 375 F.

2. In a bowl, dice the tomatoes, mix in balsamic vinegar, chopped basil, garlic, salt, pepper, and olive oil, set aside.

3. Slice the baguette into 16-18 slices and for about 10 minutes, place on a baking pan to bake.

4. Serve with warm bread slices and enjoy.

5. For leftovers, store in an airtight container and put in the fridge.

Try putting them over grilled chicken, it is amazing!

Nutrition Info: Calories: 57, Fat:2.5 g, Carbs:7.9 g, Protein:1.4 g, Sugars:0.2 g, Sodium:261 mg

Cinnamon Pancakes With Coconut *Servings: 2*

Cooking Time: 18 Minutes

Ingredients:

2 organic eggs

1 tbsp almond flour

2oz cream cheese

¼ cup shredded coconut and more for garnishing ½ tbsp erythritol

1/8 tsp salt

1 tsp cinnamon

4 tbsp stevia

½ tbsp olive oil

Directions:

1. Crack eggs in a bowl, beat until fluffy and then beat in flour and cream cheese until smooth.

2. Add remaining ingredients and then stir until well combined.

3. Take a frying pan, place it over medium heat, grease it with oil, then pour in half of the batter and cook for 3 to 4 minutes per side until the pancake has cooked and nicely golden brown.

4. Transfer pancake to a plate and cook another pancake in the same manner by using the remaining batter.

5. Sprinkle coconut on top of cooked pancakes and serve.

Nutrition Info: Calories 575, Total Fat 51g, Total Carbs 3.5g, Protein 19g

Nutty Blueberry Banana Oatmeal *Servings: 6*

Cooking Time: 2 Hours

Ingredients:

2 cup rolled eats

1/4 cup almonds (toasted)

1/4 cup walnuts

1/4 cup pecans

2 tbsp ground flax seeds

1 tsp ground ginger

1 tsp cinnamon

1/4 tsp sea salt

2 tbsp coconut sugar

½ tsp baking powder

2 cups of milk

2 bananas

1 cup fresh blueberries

1 tbsp maple syrup

1 tsp vanilla extract

1 tbsp melted butter

Yogurt for serving

Directions:

1. In a large bowl, add nuts, flax seeds, baking powder, spices, and coconut sugar and mix.

2. In another bowl, beat eggs, milk, maple syrup, and vanilla extract.

3. Slice the bananas in half and layer them in the slow cooker pot with blueberries.

4. Add oats mixture and pour the milk mixture on the top.

5. Drizzle with melted butter,

6. Cook the slow cooker on low heat for 4 hours or on high heat for 4 hours. Cook till the liquid is absorbed and oats are golden brown.

7. Serve warm and top it off with plain Greek yogurt.

Nutrition Info: Calories 346 mg Total Fat: 15g Carbohydrates: 45g Protein: 11g Sugar: 17g Fiber 7g Sodium: 145 mg Cholesterol: 39mg

Poached Salmon Egg Toast Servings: 2

Cooking Time: 4 Minutes

Ingredients:

Bread, two slices rye or whole-grain toasted Lemon juice, one quarter teaspoon

Avocado, two tablespoons mashed

Black pepper, one quarter teaspoon

Eggs, two poached

Salmon, smoked, four ounces

Scallions, one tablespoon sliced thin

Salt, one eighth teaspoon

Directions:

1. Add lemon juice to avocado with pepper and salt. Spread the mixed avocado over the toasted bread slices. Lay smoked salmon over toast and top with a poached egg. Top with sliced scallions.

Nutrition Info: Calories 389 fat 17.2 grams protein 33.5 grams carbs 31.5 grams sugar 1.3 grams fiber 9.3 grams

Chia Breakfast Pudding _Servings: 2_

Cooking Time: 0 Minutes

Ingredients:

Chia seeds, four tablespoons

Almond butter, one tablespoon

Coconut milk, three-fourths cup

Cinnamon, one teaspoon

Vanilla, one teaspoon

Cold coffee, three-fourths cup

Directions:

1. Combine all of the fixings well and pour them into a refrigerator-safe container. Cover well and let refrigerate overnight.

Nutrition Info: Calories 282 carbs 5 grams protein 5.9 grams fat 24 grams

Eggs With Cheese Servings: 1

Ingredients:

¼ c. chopped tomato

1 egg white

1 chopped green onion

2 tbsps. Fat-free milk

1 slice whole wheat bread

1 egg

½ oz. reduced fat grated cheddar cheese

Directions:

1. Mix the egg and egg whites in a bowl and add the milk.

2. Scramble the mixture in a non-stick frying pan until the eggs cook.

3. Meanwhile, toast the bread.

4. Spoon the scrambled egg mixture onto the toasted bread and top with the cheese until it melts.

5. Add the onion and the tomato.

Nutrition Info: Calories: 251, Fat:11.0 g, Carbs:22.3 g, Protein:16.9 g, Sugars:1.8 g, Sodium:451 mg

Tropical Bowls Servings: 2

Cooking Time: 0 Minutes

Ingredients:

1 cup orange juice

1 cup mango, peeled and cubed

1 cup pineapple, peeled and cubed

1 banana, peeled

1 teaspoon chia seeds

A pinch of turmeric powder

4 strawberries, sliced

Directions:

1. In your blender, mix the orange juice with the mango, pineapple, banana, chia seeds and turmeric. Pulse well, divide into bowls, top each with the strawberries and serve.

2. Enjoy!

Nutrition Info: calories 171, fat 3, fiber 6, carbs 8, protein 11

Tex-mex Hash Browns *Servings: 4*

Cooking Time: 30 Minutes

Ingredients:

1 ½ lb. potatoes, sliced into cubes

1 tablespoon olive oil

Pepper to taste

1 onion, chopped

1 red bell pepper, chopped

1 jalapeno, sliced into rings

1 teaspoon oil

½ teaspoon ground cumin

½ teaspoon taco seasoning mix

Directions:

1. Preheat your air fryer to 320 degrees F.

2. Toss potatoes in 1 tablespoon oil.

3. Season with pepper.

4. Transfer to the air fryer basket.

5. Air fry for 20 minutes, shaking twice during cooking.

6. Combine remaining ingredients in a bowl.

7. Add to the air fryer.

8. Mix well.

9. Cook at 356 degrees F for 10 minutes.

Shirataki Pasta With Avocado And Cream

Servings: 2

Cooking Time: 6 Minutes

Ingredients:

½ packet of shirataki noodles, cooked

½ of an avocado

½ tsp cracked black pepper

½ tsp salt

½ tsp dried basil

1/8 cup heavy cream

Directions:

1. Place a medium pot half full with water over medium heat, bring it to boil, then add noodles and cook for 2 minutes.

2. Then drain the noodles and set aside until required.

3. Place avocado in a bowl, mash it with a fork, 4. Mash avocado in a bowl, transfer it in a blender, add remaining ingredients, and pulse until smooth.

5. Take a frying pan, place it over medium heat and when hot, add noodles in it, pour in the avocado mixture, stir well and cook for 2

minutes until hot.

6. Serve straight away.

Nutrition Info: Calories 131, Total Fat 12.6g, Total Carbs 4.9g, Protein 1.2g, Sugar 0.3g, Sodium 588mg

Delicious Amaranth Porridge *Servings: 2*

Cooking Time: 30 Minutes

Ingredients:

½ cup water

1 cup almond milk, unsweetened

½ cup amaranth

1 pear, peeled and cubed

½ teaspoon ground cinnamon

¼ teaspoon fresh ginger, grated

A pinch of ground nutmeg

1 teaspoon maple syrup

2 tablespoons chopped pecans

Directions:

1. Put the water and the almond milk in a pot, bring to a simmer over medium heat, add the amaranth, mix and cook for 20 minutes.

Add the pear, cinnamon, ginger, nutmeg and maple syrup and mix.

Simmer for 10 minutes more, divide into bowls and serve with pecans sprinkled on top.

2. Enjoy!

Nutrition Info: calories 199, fat 9, fiber 4, carbs 25, protein 3

Almond Flour Pancakes With Cream Cheese

Servings: 2

Cooking Time: 18 Minutes

Ingredients:

½ cup almond flour

1 tsp erythritol

½ tsp cinnamon

2oz cream cheese

2 organic eggs

1 tbsp unsalted butter

Directions:

1. Prepare the pancake batter, and for this, place flour in a blender, add remaining ingredients and pulse for 2 minutes until smooth.

2. Tip the batter in a bowl and let it rest for 3 minutes.

3. Then take a large skillet pan, place it over medium heat, add butter and when it melts, pour in ¼ of prepared pancake batter.

4. Spread the batter evenly in the pan, cook for 2 minutes per side until nicely golden brown and then transfer pancake to a plate.

5. Cook three more pancakes in the same manner by using the remaining batter and, when done, serve the pancakes with favorite berries.

Nutrition Info: Calories 170, Total Fat 14.3g, Total Carbs 4.3, Protein 6.9g, Sugar 0.2g, Sodium 81mg

Turkey Apple Breakfast Hash _Servings: 5_

Cooking Time: 10 Minutes

Ingredients:

For the meat:

1 lb. ground turkey

1 tablespoon coconut oil

½ teaspoon dried thyme

½ teaspoon cinnamon

sea salt, to taste

For the hash:

1 tbsp coconut oil

1 onion

1 large apple, peeled, cored, and chopped

2 cups spinach or greens of choice

½ tsp turmeric

½ tsp dried thyme

sea salt, to taste

1 large or 2 small zucchinis

½ cup shredded carrots

2 cups cubed frozen butternut squash (or the sweet potato) 1 tsp cinnamon

¾ tsp powdered ginger

½ tsp garlic powder

Directions:

1. In a skillet, heat a spoonful of coconut oil over medium/high heat.

Attach turkey to the ground and cook until crispy. Season with thyme, cinnamon, and a pinch of sea salt. Move to the plate.

2. Throw remaining coconut oil into the same skillet and sauté onion until softened for 2-3 minutes.

3. Add the courgettes, apple, carrots, and frozen squash to taste—

Cook for around 4-5 minutes, or until veggies soften.

4. Attach and whisk in spinach until wilted.

5. Add cooked turkey, seasoning, salt, and shut off oil.

6. Enjoy this hash fresh from the pan, or let it cool and refrigerate all week long. The hash can remain in a sealed container in the

refrigerator for about 5-6 days.

Nutrition Info: Calories 350 Carbs: 20g Fat: 19g Protein: 28g

Cheesy Flax And Hemp Seeds Muffins Servings: 2

Cooking Time: 30 Minutes

Ingredients:

1/8 cup flax seeds meal

¼ cup raw hemp seeds

¼ cup almond meal

Salt, to taste

¼ tsp baking powder

3 organic eggs, beaten

1/8 cup nutritional yeast flakes

¼ cup cottage cheese, low-fat

¼ cup grated parmesan cheese

¼ cup scallion, sliced thinly

1 tbsp olive oil

Directions:

1. Switch on the oven, then set it 360°F and let it preheat.

2. Meanwhile, take two ramekins, grease them with oil, and set aside until required.

3. Take a medium bowl, add flax seeds, hemp seeds, and almond meal, and then stir in salt and baking powder until mixed.

4. Crack eggs in another bowl, add yeast, cottage cheese, and parmesan, stir well until combined, and then stir this mixture into the almond meal mixture until incorporated.

5. Fold in scallions, then distribute the mixture between prepared ramekins and bake for 30 minutes until muffins are firm and the top is nicely golden brown.

6. When done, take out the muffins from the ramekins and let them cool completely on a wire rack.

7. For meal prepping, wrap each muffin with a paper towel and refrigerate for up to thirty-four days.

8. When ready to eat, reheat muffins in the microwave until hot and then serve.

Nutrition Info: Calories 179, Total Fat 10.9g, Total Carbs 6.9g, Protein 15.4g, Sugar 2.3g, Sodium 311mg

Cheesy Cauliflower Waffles With Chives

Servings: 2

Cooking Time: 15 Minutes

Ingredients:

1 cup cauliflower florets

1 tbsp chives, minced

½ tsp cracked black pepper

1 tsp onion powder

1 tsp garlic powder

1 cup shredded mozzarella cheese

½ cup grated parmesan cheese

2 organic eggs, beaten

1 tbsp olive oil

Directions:

1. Switch on the waffle iron, grease it with oil and let it preheat.

2. Meanwhile, prepare the waffle batter and for this, place all its ingredients in a bowl and whisk until combined.

3. Ladle half of the batter into the hot waffle iron, shut it with lid, and cook until nicely golden brown.

4. Take out the waffle and cook another waffle in the same manner by using the remaining batter.

5. For meal prepping, place waffles in an airtight container, separating waffles with a wax paper and store for up to four days.

Nutrition Info: Calories 149, Total Fat 8.5g, Total Carbs 6.1g, Protein 13.3g, Sugar 2.3g, Sodium 228mg

Breakfast Sandwich Servings: 1

Cooking Time: 7 Minutes

Ingredients:

1 frozen breakfast

Directions:

1. Air fry sandwich at 340 degrees F for 7 minutes.

106. Savory Veggie Muffins Servings: 5

Cooking Time: 18-23 Minutes

Ingredients:

¾ cup almond meal

½ tsp baking soda

¼ cup whey Protein concentrate powder

2 teaspoons fresh dill, chopped

Salt, to taste

4 large organic eggs

1½ tablespoons nutritional yeast

2 teaspoons apple cider vinegar

3 tablespoons fresh lemon juice

2 tablespoons coconut oil, melted

1 cup coconut butter, softened

1 bunch scallion, chopped

2 medium carrots, peeled and grated

½ cup fresh parsley, chopped

Directions:

1. Preheat the oven to 350 degrees F. Grease 10 cups of your large muffin tin.

2. In a large bowl, mix together flour, baking soda, Protein powder and salt.

3. In another bowl, add eggs, nutritional yeast, vinegar, lemon juice and oil and beat till well combined.

4. Add coconut butter and beat till mixture becomes smooth.

5. Add egg mixture into flour mixture and mix till well combined.

6. Fold in scallion, carts and parsley.

7. Place the amalgamation into prepared muffin cups evenly.

8. Bake for about 18-23 minutes or till a toothpick inserted inside center comes out clean.

Nutrition Info: Calories: 378, Fat: 13g, Carbohydrates: 32g, Fiber: 11g, Protein: 32g

Zucchini Pancakes Servings: 8

Cooking Time: 6-10 Min

Ingredients:

1 cup chickpea flour

1½ cups water, divided

¼ teaspoon cumin seeds

¼ tsp cayenne

¼ teaspoon ground turmeric

Salt, to taste

½ cup zucchini, shredded

½ cup red onion, chopped finely

1 green chile, seeded and chopped finely

¼ cup fresh cilantro, chopped

Directions:

1. In a large bowl, add flour and ¾ cup with the water and beat till smooth.

2. Add remaining water and beat till a thin 3. Fold inside onion, ginger, Serrano pepper and cilantro.

4. Lightly, grease a substantial nonstick skillet with oil and heat on medium-low heat.

5. Add about ¼ cup of mixture and tilt the pan to spread it evenly in the skillet.

6. Cook for around 4-6 minutes.

7. Carefully, alter the side and cook for approximately 2-4 minutes.

8. Repeat while using remaining mixture.

9. Serve together with your desired topping.

Nutrition Info: Calories: 389, Fat: 13g, Carbohydrates: 25g, Fiber: 4g, Protein: 21g

Breakfast Burgers With Avocado Buns _Servings: 1_

Cooking Time: 5 Minutes

Ingredients:

1 ripe avocado

1 egg, pasture-raised

1 red onion slice

1 tomato slice

1 lettuce leaf

Sesame seed for garnish

Salt to taste

Directions:

1. Peel the avocado and remove the seed. Slice the avocado into half. This will serve as the bun. Set aside.

2. Grease a skillet over medium flame and fry the egg's sunny side up for 5 minutes or until set.

3. Assemble the breakfast burger by placing on top of one avocado half with the egg, red onion, tomato, and lettuce leaf.

4. Top with the remaining avocado bun.

5. Garnish with sesame seeds on top and season with salt to taste.

Nutrition Info: Calories 458Total Fat 39gSaturated Fat 4gTotal Carbs 20gNet Carbs 6g,Protein 13gSugar: 8gFiber: 14gSodium: 118mgPotassium 1184mg

Tasty Cheesy And Creamy Spinach Puffs

Servings: 2

Cooking Time: 12 Minutes

Ingredients:

½ cup almond flour

½ tsp garlic powder

½ tsp salt

1 organic egg

1½ tbsp heavy whipping cream

¼ cup feta cheese, crumbled

½ tbsp olive oil

Directions:

1. Switch on the oven, then set its temperature to 350 °F and let it preheat.

2. Meanwhile, prepare the cookie batter, and for this, place all the ingredients in a blender and then pulse for 2 minutes until smooth.

3. Prepare cookies and for this, place prepared batter onto a working space and then shape it with 1-inch balls.

4. Take a cookie sheet, grease it with oil, then arrange cookies on it, with some distance apart, and bake for 12 minutes until cooked and nicely golden.

5. When done, let cookies cool in the cookie sheet for 5 minutes, then transfer them onto a wire rack to cool completely and then serve.

Nutrition Info: Calories 294, Total Fat 24g, Total Carbs 7.8g, Protein 12.2g, Sugar 1.1g, Sodium 840mg

www.ingramcontent.com/pod-product-compliance
Lightning Source LLC
Chambersburg PA
CBHW071819080526
44589CB00012B/854